DATE			
APR 17 '80			
NOV 1 1 '92			
DEC 0 2 '92			

Classics In
Child Development

Classics In
Child Development

Advisory Editors

JUDITH KRIEGER GARDNER
HOWARD GARDNER

Editorial Board

THE FIRST YEAR
OF LIFE

by Charlotte Bühler

ARNO PRESS

A New York Times Company

New York — 1975

Reprint Edition 1975 by Arno Press Inc.

Reprinted from a copy in
  The University of Illinois Library

Classics in Child Development
ISBN for complete set: 0-405-06450-0
See last pages of this volume for titles.

Manufactured in the United States of America

———◆———

Library of Congress Cataloging in Publication Data

Buhler, Charlotte Malachowski, 1893-
    The first year of life.

    (Classics in child development)
    Translation of Inventar der Verhaltungsweisen des er-
sten Lebensjahres.
    Reprint of the ed. published by John Day Co., New
York.
    Bibliography: p.
    1. Infant psychology. I. Title. II. Series.
BF723.I6B8313 1975   155.4'22   74-21402
ISBN 0-405-06455-1

THE FIRST YEAR
OF LIFE

THE FIRST YEAR OF LIFE

by Charlotte Bühler

TRANSLATED BY
Pearl Greenberg & Rowena Ripin

THE JOHN DAY COMPANY
New York

ABOUT THE AUTHOR

CHARLOTTE BÜHLER, who studied at the University of München and the University of Berlin, is at present professor of child psychology at the University of Vienna and is associated also with her husband, Karl Bühler, at the Psychological Institute of Vienna. She is the author of a number of books and articles on psychology published in Germany and Austria, and is associate editor of the *Journal of Genetic Psychology* and of the *Genetic Psychology Monographs.*

PREFACE

THE appearance of the first English translation of one of Charlotte Bühler's books on child psychology is an event of scientific significance and importance. The psychological world has long known and justly respected the earnest and fruitful experimental work that is being carried on in Vienna and has accorded it a foremost place among the great researches of to-day. The choice of the present volume, *The First Year of Life,* as an introduction to Charlotte Bühler's work is a fortunate one; for not only is it one of the most fundamental of her books, but also it presents the essence of her procedures and her method and demonstrates the logical and convincing way in which she draws her inferences from the data.

The laboratory work on which this book is based was carried out in that already famous institution, "Kinderübernahmsstelle der Gemeinde Wien." There Dr. Bühler with her small group of assistants performed the tasks required with scientific detachment and unwearying persistence. Day and night they sat by the side of the child or peered through the glass that forms the walls of the Kinderübernahmsstelle. They carried on this work with a conviction of the precision of their technique and the accuracy of their observations, and further, in the belief that a normal day cycle could be determined. *The First Year of Life* is the outcome of this labor—a work which despite the prolific psychological investigations of recent times has

vii

for five years stood alone, an authoritative research.

It is impossible to speak of the Psychological Institute of Vienna without acknowledging the important part taken by Dr. Hildegard Hetzer, assistant to Dr. Bühler. Dr. Hetzer directs the experimental work and is responsible for the accuracy and completeness of the findings.

The tests are the particular contribution of Fr. Käthe Wolf. She planned the experiments and did the laboratory work in connection with them. They are the natural and expected corollary of the "normal day cycle," testing and proving that initial work at the same time. Recent retesting in Vienna has demonstrated the validity of the tests, and they are at the present time being tried out in American child research institutions.

The First Year of Life appeared originally as *Inventar der Verhaltungsweisen des ersten Lebensjahres* by Charlotte Bühler and Hildegard Hetzer in *Quellen und Studien zur Jugendkunde*, Heft 5, Jena, Gustav Fischer, 1927. The *Babytests* by Hildegard Hetzer and Käthe Wolf appeared in *Die Zeitschrift für Psychologie*, volume 107, 1928. Tests for the second year of life, *Eine Testreihe für das zweite Lebensjahr*, are by Hildegard Hetzer and Ludwig Koller.

The translation adheres very closely to the original text. Departures have been made only in a few cases where it was deemed to be essential for clarity.

PEARL GREENBERG,
ROWENA RIPIN.

CONTENTS

PART I

THE FIRST YEAR OF LIFE

TRANSLATION BY PEARL GREENBERG

ix

Contents

PART II

THE TESTS FOR THE FIRST AND
SECOND YEAR OF LIFE

TRANSLATION BY ROWENA RIPIN

PART I
THE FIRST YEAR OF LIFE

CHAPTER I

Statement of the Problem and of the Method

W. BECHTEREW and A. Gesell were among the first to make a study, in inventory fashion, of the earliest ways of behavior in children. It was their aim to obtain a general view of the problems in the life of a child, as completely as possible. Working toward this end Gesell made some very exact studies of children and does indeed give examples of continuous observations—24 hours in length—of a two months old and of a six months old child. In Bechterew's Institute, Denissova and Figurin observed two newborn children, from birth on, by day and by night, for nine days.

The intention underlying our observations went even further. In the first place it was our aim to obtain a complete picture of the child's behavior during the first year of life. But further, we wished, by means of a very exhaustive inventory of every item of observable behavior, to obtain a characteristic inventory of one that would serve as a standard for average and normal development within this period.

The method employed was that of uninterrupted systematic observation of one and the same child under those conditions which were normal in his everyday life. The child under observation was watched, whether waking or sleeping, over a period of twenty-four hours by observers who relieved each other at eight-hour intervals. The periods of observation were begun at different times of the day with the different subjects. The observer kept himself completely passive in relation to the child. He sat at the side of the child and in no way disturbed the normal daily plan. He at no time left the child, even when the child slept. And he kept accurate record of all that he observed. As often as a new behavior occurred the precise time of its occurrence was noted. Where unusual precision was necessary because of the variability of the periods, a stop watch was used.

Even at night normal and customary conditions prevailed. The children lay in a darkened room and only a very faint light fell on them so that one could continue to perceive even the slightest change in conduct. This was the normal light for those children who were in the *Kinderübernahmsstelle*[1]—they were the largest percentage of the children observed in this investigation. The observer tried to avoid any disturbance of the child's sleep and, during the night, was, as a rule, separated from the child by the glass wall of the room in which the child lived. Whenever light was required for writing, the observer used a small electrical flashlight which he was careful not to reflect on the child. Each perceptible change in the childish behavior was noted and recorded so far as the means of descriptive language was able to represent them. It was found that we came very soon to the limit of language as a means of representation for impulsive moments and for vocalization, and in our later research we have made use of a finer method of observation and representation.

Since the observer did not permit the introduction of any artificial stimulus, there is lacking in our inventory whole groups of reactions which could have been

[1] Reception House for Children in Vienna.

invoked by the experimental method. I recall, for example, the experimental work of Kusmal (and the work of others) who brought about reactions to taste. Such experiments (in our opinion) fail to have any scientific value.

In order to avoid the possible errors that might have occurred had the observations been carried on by a larger number of workers, the greatest part of these protocols were taken by the same two observers. These had previously agreed, in complete detail, upon the method and the terminology.

In all, sixty-nine children of the first year of life were observed, there being always five children of each month. Of these, 40 per cent were children from private homes and 60 per cent were "institution" children. Table I gives the age, sex, and number of the children observed.

TABLE I

Age, Sex and Number of the Observed Children

Age.....	0;0	0;1	0;2	0;3	0;4	0;5	0;6	0;7	0;8	0;9	0;10	0;11	1;0	Total
Child No.	*B1	B5	G11	G16	B20	B26	G30	G34	G39	B44	G49	G54	B56	
	B2	B6	G12	B12	G21	G27	G31	B35	B40	B45	B50	G55	G57	
	B3	B7	G13	G17	G22	G28	G32	G36	B41	B46	G51	G39	B58	
	B4	B8	G14	G23	B23	G29	B33	B37	B42	B47	B52	B60	B59	
		B9	G15	G24	G24	G22	G22	B38	B48	G48	B53	B63	B61	
		B2		G25	G25				G30					
		B10												
Boys....	4	7	—	1	2	1	1	3	4	3	3	2	4	35
Girls	—	—	5	5	4	4	4	2	2	2	2	3	1	34
Total....	4	7	5	6	6	5	5	5	6	5	5	5	5	69

* B = boy.   G = girl.

By "children of private homes" we mean first of all those children who were observed in their home environment, and secondly those children who came to the *Kinderübernahmsstelle* with their mothers. The remaining children under observation were largely children who came out of the family care to spend a three-week quarantine period in the *Kinderübernahmsstelle* before being placed either with a foster mother or in some other institution. They were, therefore, in no way typical institutional children. Moreover, since these children came from a very varied social milieu, there was no need to fear that the material was in any way onesided. A few errors in observation, illness on the part of the children, and similar conditions decreased the number of records. With the exception of the first group (the newborn) there were always five complete observations made in each age-group. Since the children were not always the desired age precisely to the day, an allowance for a range of fourteen days was made. Accordingly, a child either a week older or younger than one month was reckoned as one month. There was only one exception made, and that was with a group of newborn babies. This group consisted of four children from one to ten days of age, with an average age of five days (o; o [+ 5]).[2] This standard for "newborn" appears to be even medically correct, for a child is considered "newborn" until those signs disappear which remind one that the child is not a self-reliant organism—that is, until the navel heals. All children were examined medically before the investigations were begun, and only healthy babies were used as subjects of observation.

Their average weight, which gives some evidence

[2] The device for representing the child age o; o (+ 5) reads: no years, no months and five days. This system will be used throughout this text.

of their physical condition, did not vary essentially from the normal expected weight. This is shown in Table II.

TABLE II

The Average Weight of Observed Children *

Age	0;0	0;1	0;2	0;3	0;4	0;5	0;6	0;7	0;8	0;9	0;10	0;11	1;0
Normal or Expected Weight †.	6.61	7.71	8.81	9.91	11.01	12.11	13.22	14.32	15.41	16.52	17.61	18.72	19.19
Actual Weight..		8.02	8.27	8.40	11.25	11.35	12.93	16.09	16.41	17.89	17.92	18.26	18.83	19.26

* Calculated in pounds from the data given in grams in the original Table II in the Inventar.

† According to the statistics of Dr. Clemens Pirquet and the American Red Cross.

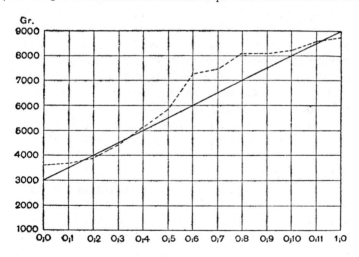

CHART 1. Average weight of observed children (in grams).
————— expected weight (according to Pirquet).
-------- actual weight.

7

The First Year of Life

The observations were carried out in the months of January to April, 1926. It is to be noticed that several times the same children were observed at different age-levels so that the monthly progress in development could be seen in the case of one and the same child. The time spent on actual observation amounts, in round numbers, to about 1,620 hours. The protocols themselves fill 922 closely written pages.

From the point of view of our main problem, it is possible to treat the assembled material in three directions. First, the *qualitative* and *quantitative* analysis of the behavior; second, the time analysis of the day and the time measurement of the behavior; and third, *the meaning of the facts*—the establishment of the levels of development in the course of the first year of life. The qualitative and quantitative analysis of the behavior describes and determines the separate behaviors at the different age-levels. Such an analysis establishes how the various ways of behavior modify themselves during the first year of life; it makes clear which behaviors disappear and substitute each other, which new one enters, etc. Such an analysis finally counts the many-sidedness of the series of reactions which are to be found in the different individuals at different age-levels. The second problem is concerned with those ways of behavior which can be observed within the limit of one day, and with separating and determining those groups of reactions which follow one upon the other. The second problem includes also a consideration of the daily time value to be appointed to the different groups of behaviors found in each age-level. By daily value is meant the duration (in time) of a definite group of behavior observed within the period of twenty-four hours. The day values of different age-levels can be compared with one another, and many and important items of value can be studied and collected.

From all these facts, obtained through the two-fold analysis, it was possible to differentiate the development in definite periods and to establish the levels of development in the first year of life.

The Units of Behavior

THE main question in this work is: How does one take the record—what are the data to be quoted and collected? Let us begin the discussion of this question, which has a great theoretical and practical importance, by giving a few concrete examples. Suppose you have in front of you three children at the ages of two, five, and eight months. You put a towel on the face of each child and observe their reactions. You will find that the youngest, displaying all the movements he is able to produce, tries with all means to get rid of the towel. The whole set of reflexes from top to toe is roused. At the same time the child may cry. But despite all his efforts he is not and cannot be successful. The second child will develop organized and directed movements instead of the chaotic and undirected reflex reaction. He will grasp with his hands in the direction of the towel and sometimes, though with much effort and pain, he will even be successful in drawing it away. The oldest child (eight months), however, will show neither effort nor pain, but will grasp and draw the towel away, maybe even in a laughing and playful manner. His movements are not only organized but at the same time straight and easy. And what was pain and trouble for the younger ones has now become play and joy. These are the three cases. I come back now to

[1] This chapter is not a translation from the original, but a new formulation for the English edition of the book.

my question which I raised and I ask, "How shall we take the record; and how shall we collect and classify the data of these three situations and responses."

So far, only one ideal of objective description has been emphasized, and that most radically by Bechterew and Watson. This method is to give a complete enumeration of all reflexes which are displayed by the child in the whole situation. The result in this case would be a list of all the single movements within the sequence of the whole process. Even supposing this would be possible, we would have at the end a table which would enumerate and score so many hundred of reflexes of all possible kinds—that is, when studying the youngest child. Then in the second child, you would find a considerable decrease of reflexes but an increase of organized movements; and there would probably be a further increase of motor coördination in the third child. In addition to this, a complete record would take in the reactions of crying and laughing and also, of course, the duration of the reaction.

Now suppose we had such tables of all the reactions, during the whole day, with natural situations—tables which would enumerate and score and show the total of reflexes, coördinated movements, and durations. Would that in itself be of any psychological interest? It would certainly not and there is no psychologist in the world who is satisfied with these tables as such, though some psychologists emphasize the fact that they are giving nothing more than the objective facts of the process or behavior displayed in front of them. In fact, not one of them does really state a complete list of reflexes. Bechterew as well as Watson group the facts of observation and with that grouping, of course, they begin to interpret them. Now, what is the effect of this grouping?

Let us imagine a long tabulation listing all the motor reactions of the day made by one child. Bechterew would take all the reactions of the towel situation together and would say that all this was a defense reaction. That means he would take, as he says, the dominant of such a set of motor reactions, and the dominant would be the feature which they all have in common. Now with this emphasis on a dominant, the continuous flow of behavior is provided with a center, and is grouped through interpretation. This group becomes the unit of one performance. And only then do the facts attain a psychological significance. Of course this same procedure would be true for the units of emotion as Watson, or the units of instinctive behavior as Thorndike points them out. This fact has been discussed and elaborated by Karl Bühler.

We can go further. Considerable doubt has been raised as to whether there are any single reflexes, movements, and impulses; and whether they can be isolated and separated from each other, as they sometimes appear to be. But on the contrary, it is the belief of some psychologists, as W. Koehler and his group emphasize, that it is the psychophysical system as a whole which reacts to the situation. Goldstein and Lewin have given concrete examples of individual cases and explain how they are to be understood according to the conception of the Gestalt-psychology. According to Goldstein's thinking, the stimulus—as, for instance, the towel in our experiment—causes an excitation of the whole organism. This excitation has a certain distribution and with that the organism is in a specific tension, which has to be resolved. With the so-called reaction, a new balance is constituted.

In this conception the single movement, as such, has lost every interest and is only to be conceived as part of a configuration. Not only through interpretation and the psychologist's grouping, but in the reality, therefore, the unit is the reaction with all the movements observed. With this conception, we should have the right to take the whole as a fact and so refer to the single parts of it only in so far as we may be interested in them.

But in what now are we really interested, if we take an inventory of the child's development? I think there is one feature which as yet has not been discussed at all, and that is the success or the failure of the efforts to reach their ends. Is not this relationship of means and ends, or the outcome of success and failure of certain behaviors within the situation, the main factor of our psychological interest? If we agree with that, any record which refers only to movements of the child is of no use, because it is quite incomplete. Instead of this, we should need a record which also would include the changes that take place in the object in the situation with which the child is concerned in the reaction. Suppose the child manipulate with a pencil, the effect of this manipulation would be as important a fact for the psychologist as the movements of manipulation. More than that, only in connection with this effect, are the movements of psychological interest. In other words, only in relationship to its effect or success, does a process attain psychological significance. This very important fact was realized some years ago by Thorndike when he pointed out situation, response, and effect as three basic psychological features. This unit of behavior with its effect, success, or failure, we will call an act or performance. And what really interests us is how the effect is bound up with its preceding behavior. The details of the behavior interest us only in so far as they may be essential in explaining the effect.

Applied to a concrete example: For the understanding of the child's development, it seems very important to us to see how the child masters a difficult situation of life. In this connection it seems of extreme interest that we are able to show stages of this mastery over a simple obstacle: a first stage where the child never succeeds; a second stage, where he succeeds sometimes and with effort; and a third stage, where the child is successful always and with ease. To understand this, the lack of coördination, as well as the degree of coördination in the movements of the child, seemed to us to be of importance; not, however, the listing of each single reflex movement, enumerating and scoring them. Thus it was that we observed the child's behavior from the viewpoint of performance which was to be recognized and scored. So we worked out a scheme of performances.

As a matter of fact, the two other investigators in the field of observational study and inventory, Gesell and Bechterew, have to a certain degree arrived at the same viewpoint, in their practice. When Gesell compares two children, he in fact compares them in their ability to perform certain things. And what he calls in his introduction "behavior items" are mostly not only behaviors but indeed performances. The categories of the figures are only a classification scheme for functions, for processes, while later on the comparison is made in performances, which proves to be the much more successful and productive viewpoint. The same can be shown with Bechterew and his group. Though in principle and in the planning, which was formulated ahead of the studies, the viewpoint of reflexes is emphasized, the classification ends with such headlines as "attack" and "defense." So that we can say that performance is really the only viewpoint which fully describes behavior.

CHAPTER III

The Positive and Negative Reactions

BECAUSE of its very nature the organism of the human being reacts positively to the influences which are beneficial to it, and negatively to those influences which are harmful to it. This reaction is, moreover, a primary and basic one, and must be considered so in spite of the fact that later complications enter the situation which modify the elementary aspect of this behavior. These modifications are twofold. In the first place they arise from the fact that, in the living organism, the reaction of a single organ or of a group of organs can be substituted for, can take the place of, the reaction of the organism as a whole. It can therefore happen that the reactions of the single organ, or of the group of organs, can come into conflict with each other. For example, the nerves of taste can react positively to a material which is harmful to the gastrointestinal tract. In other words, we can enjoy eating something which may be difficult to digest. In this case stimulation is no longer either simply beneficial or simply harmful, nor is the reaction directly in response to the harmfulness or beneficiality of the stimulus. The generally accepted idea that the organism always reacts positively to a stimulus which is beneficial—at least in its final result—contains, upon closer examination, much that is incorrect.

The second type of complication occurs through the fact that the central nervous system can bring about

general directions which may be in conflict with the reactions of specific and single organs. Let us take the
case of a young boy who smokes. This boy's nerves of
smell and of taste as well as those of his whole organism may react absolutely negatively to cigarettes.
Yet he smokes. He seems impelled to do so by a sort
of ambition which his will determines. In short, the
positive and negative reactions of the higher organism,
especially of the human being, are a complicated system, and that action which at last really does take place
is, in fact, only the last link of a chain of part-reactions.
Many of these are repressed from the very beginning.

There are still further complications to be taken into
consideration. We must give thought to the contradic-
tions and interdependencies which are to be found in
the fully mature individual. At that stage of development in which human beings are already highly organized, the reactions are no longer entirely positive or
negative, and the emotions and impulses accompanying
them are likewise composites both of pleasure and displeasure, of sympathy and antipathy. This whole emotional process is, of course, not to be considered as a
meaningless phenomenon, attendant upon the reactions;
but both are together considered as a system of motor
and inhibitor. This conception, that of motor and inhibitor, has been developed by Karl Bühler, under the
title, *The Hedonalgic Reaction*. We wish here to add
several considerations.

Let us consider a very primitive organism such as a
sponge whose pores are opened so as to take in nourishment through the mechanical stimulation brought
about by flowing water. Here we find that no inner
motor is necessary in order that the absorption of food
be set into motion. If we consider instead an organism

which must make many painstaking movements in order to obtain its nourishment, then we can understand the need for a strong inner motor to bring about the movements necessary for the searching of food. In this case the discomfort accompanying the need of nourishment acts as the motor. We can go further. Whenever the process of obtaining food ends by a simple and automatic means, that is, when the receptor is filled, then the organism needs no indication when to cease. When such is not the case, however, and a harmful overabundance of nourishment must be avoided, then pleasure enters as soon as a condition of optimal satisfaction is reached. And pleasure, as such, occurs in order that the endeavor of finding nourishment should cease.

This entrance of pleasure into the feeding situation in order that further seeking of nourishment should cease can be observed in children. At least, we see that satisfaction in feeding produces the first expression of comfort in the child. It would seem, therefore, that in the early stages of development, displeasure can be the motor which causes positive as well as negative reactions; pleasure is only the inhibitor of movement. Later on, through the memory of a recalled pleasant situation, pleasure can be anticipated, and this acts as a motor for positive action. In the same way remembered displeasure acts as a motor for negative action. If this whole argumentation is correct, then it is to be understood that displeasure brings about many more reactions than does pleasure.

We mentioned at the beginning, in connection with the complexities of the reaction system, the fact that many part-reactions of the organisms were repressed, that only a few of the many stimuli and impulses led to genuine reactions.

The Positive and Negative Reactions

It is also true that in the course of development the reactions are in many ways modified. We have said, in fact, that in the place of the general movement of the entire organism there enter later part-movements—for example: a flight movement of the head, a defense movement of the hand, a grasping movement of the hand. Further, there enters, in the case of higher animals living in communities, various expressional movements in the place of, or in addition to, direct reactions. That animal, for example, who, in his repulse of danger, is not able to master the situation alone, lets out a cry of help.

In man well-nigh all direct communication has been gradually transferred to speech. And the expressional movement has remained only as a primitive sign of the intended reaction. The expressional movement reveals to us two things: the intended reaction and the emotion lying behind that reaction in either its positive or negative direction. Both—the means of the reaction and the emotional expression—belong together in our use of the term "behavior unit."

The Direction or Character of the Reaction: With this topic we come to a new fact. At the early stages of development there is unity between the direction of the movement and the character of the reaction. Both go the same way. That is, we speak of flight movements—and flight means a drawing away movement. There is also a movement toward things. This simple identity is discontinued in that very movement in which repulse and attack movements enter the behavior situation. The meaning of these movements and their forms are unlike. Repulse movements and those of attack are positive movements with a negative meaning. From then on, a positive reaction is not, without further

19

qualification, identical with a going toward movement, nor is a negative reaction always identical with a withdrawing movement. The meaning of a movement can be other than its direction. In this presentation we will seek to group the reactions according to their meaning, and not according to their direction. For us, negative reactions are all those which according to their meaning turn toward an object . . . accepting it, striving toward it, later desiring it.

CHAPTER IV

The Negatively Directed Reactions

THERE are noticeably more negative ways of behavior to be observed in newborn children than there are positive. From the very first day of life, negative expressional movements and sounds are to be noted. Positive expressional movements and sounds, on the other hand, appear for the first time, in the second month. It seems, therefore, that the sensitive and helpless bodies of newborn children encounter decidedly more situations from which to flee than to seek, and probably also they encounter much more displeasure than pleasure.

1. FLIGHT AND DEFENSE MOVEMENTS. We must make a distinction between flight and defense movements. We have already characterized the defense movements as being more complex than flight movements. Our differentiation between defense and flight movements is, in a certain sense, in opposition to the interpretation of Bechterew. Bechterew characterizes all those movements which the child uses as a means of self-defense, as defense movements. He maintains that the flight movements can exist only in animals who have the ability of locomotion (and children do not have that ability developed). Since Bechterew classes every movement toward anything as an act of attack, he can therefore characterize attack as well as defense as a fundamental function of the organism, whereas, according to our interpretation and observa-

tion, flight and movement toward objects occur earlier than attack and defense movements.

Take, for example, the case of the cleaning of an infant's nose. This is a situation which can be observed in all children, and it is at the same time a situation in which it is possible to observe how the reaction to an outside disturbance becomes ever more specific and purposeful.

The newborn child cries and makes aimless restless movements with arms, legs, and head. A turning away of the head occurs with the infant only when he reacts to a shock—that is, to a sudden strong stimulus. In the case of the child whose nose was being cleaned, it was the contact of the cotton swab to which he reacted. A child of one month turns his head aside when receiving influence of a mild stimulus that is continued—such stimuli as the rubbing and wiping of his nose. A flight movement of the head is later accompanied by the flight movements of the arms and legs, and a rearing defense movement of the body. The change from flight to defense movement takes place in the fourth month. The moving away and throwing back of the head is then also accompanied by movements which are as yet impulsive, going often in the direction of the stimulus. These movements in many cases accidentally lead to a success—they really hinder the hand of the grownup from the continuation of a disliked cleaning. In the fifth month the defense movement of a child in such a situation becomes a real pushing away, and a six months child deters the action by firmly holding the hand of the grownup.

B 1:0;0(+ 1) Cries and makes restless movements at the cleaning of his nose.

The Negatively Directed Reactions

B 3:0;0(+ 3)   Turns his head away when the wadding first comes in contact with his face. Submits to further cleaning, but with loud cries and restless movements.

B 12:0;2   Throws back and turns away his head at cleaning of the nose. Added to that, sounds of displeasure.

G 11:0;2   Turns aside her head from the cleaning of her nose and ears. Moves her hands a little backward.

G 22:0;4   With her little hands, which were wandering over her own face, pushes aside the hand of the mother at the cleaning of the nose and ears.

B 20:0;4   Pushes both feet toward the arm of the mother, who was just cleaning the nose.

G 22:0;5   Pushes with both hands the hand of the mother who is cleaning her nose, and attempts to push the hand away.

There is still another fact worthy of attention in this connection. The child whose defense movements in this situation leave him ineffectual, will renounce defense movements and seek to wrest away from the stimulus as soon as he is able to change his position— say, at the age of eight months. He accomplishes this through a flight of his entire body—rolling about, pushing forward, and crawling away.

In the first quarter year we have observed, so far, only the flight movement. It is not altogether certain whether the shoving aside of the nipple or spitting out —when the child is satiated—admit of the same interpretation. It is more likely that they exhibit a defense reaction. This type of defense—spitting and pushing aside of the bottle nipple—is not to be observed before the end of the first month. Vomiting—an act which must likewise be considered a defense against a material thing—can be observed in newborn babies.

Altogether, one can say that very probably defense occurs earlier in connection with the taking of nourishment than in other spheres.

Concerning flight movements we can state:

NEWBORN: Moves head aside at strong sensory stimuli. Makes restless, aimless movements. Stretches sidewards and flexes his limbs.

ONE MONTH OLD CHILD: Throws head back when satiated or when senses are stimulated. Bends back and makes restless movements of the head.

END OF SECOND MONTH: Turns aside the head and single limb. Turns and rubs his back on anything lying under him.

FROM THE FIFTH MONTH ON: Uses the change of posture as a flight movement. Finally—

IN THE LAST QUARTER YEAR: We can speak of flight of the entire body. We can also observe other flight movements, aside from those which result from strong or unpleasant sensory stimulations, of which unpleasant contacts play the most important rôle. Such are the flight movements to be observed in cases of satiation, of undesired nourishment, when toys are taken away, and in connection with the reaction of fear.

Those defense and flight movements already described and discussed as not being determinate in their interpretation can be said to become definite in the fourth month. That is, by the time the child is four months old he already exhibits definite defense and definite flight movements. And he begins to add new reactions. At six months he includes shoving aside movements of the legs in his repertoire. He also begins now to depart from an earlier behavior stage in which he made these movements only when he experienced a direct bodily contact, and at the age of six and seven months he exhibits defense movements as soon as the stimulus approaches. For example, he meets the hand that holds the dreaded cotton swab for cleaning the nose while it is only half way and he holds it avertingly off. The defense movements of the eight months old child which accompany his fear reactions—his kicking, his stretching out of the hands, and lifting them in that direction in which he expects danger—are already directed toward an object which has not yet begun to do any harm.

2. SCREAMING AND CRYING SOUNDS OF DISPLEASURE. The screaming which occurs from the very first day is, at the start, a highly undifferentiated behavior. It is always closely connected with displeasure and other negative emotions, and, so far as it has meaning, it can be interpreted as negative. Whether, however, the intended reaction in behalf of which the helpless child cries is not always negative, and whether there does not exist also a crying of desire, is not to be denied without further discussion. Probably this question is, indeed, to be answered in the affirmative, as will be seen later. Modifications in the crying sounds can be observed from the second month on. Let us investigate these situations in which crying enters.

The first and most striking observation to be noted in the first half year is that *crying always occurs closely connected with movement.* We have, therefore, a unit of behavior in which the crying is "the dominant." [1] Only from the second half year on does crying also

---

[1] This terminology is taken from Uchtomsky who quotes from Bechterew "Neues aus dem Begiet der Reflexologie und Physiologie des Nerven-systems" (Russia), 1925.

occur when a child is lying quietly. Crying with tears begins only after the first month, and first of all as crying together with screaming.

The second observation to be noted is:

All causes of crying in the first four months revert back directly to bodily hurts and needs.

Even on the very first day screaming occurs in many situations which have a negative aspect. We observed this screaming in the case of pain (a pricking), sudden lifting up during sleep, cleaning of the nose, examination by the doctor, and hence, generally speaking, in the case of any direct sensitive manipulations of the body of the child.

While reverting directly to bodily needs and hurts, the causes of the child's early crying can nevertheless be further classified and even the description of the kinds of crying further defined.

(a) Screaming caused by pain. The screaming caused by lasting pain and difficulties of digestion is loud, shrill, continuous and without long pauses. From time to time it gives over into soft whimperings and groaning. Shrill, single cries, which likewise are succeeded by whimpering and groaning, are the second form of crying to be noticed in the case of continued pain. A still more undifferentiated screaming, in continued pain, was observed in the case of a newborn child from whom, through a prick wound in the heel, blood for examination was drawn. The elimination of feces likewise causes the newborn child to cry in an undifferentiated manner. At the beginning of the second month the screaming of a child begins to exhibit differences. From then on, the child cries at disturbances of digestion, at the taking of blood, and at the setting in of illness, in the manner described above.

(b) Screaming caused by strong sensory stimuli. Strong sensory stimuli, especially sudden stimuli, are often the cause of screaming. In most cases a frightened quivering precedes the screaming. Such shock influences are to be observed when the child is exposed to such stimuli as: very bright light, sharp noises, sudden contact, cleaning of the nose, drying, douching, rapid change of temperatures, effect of cold if the child is uncovered, heat in the bath. With the exception of bright light all these stimuli prove themselves effective even with the newborn child.

Child 1:0;0 (+ 1). Convulsive quivering followed by crying was observed in the following circumstances: when the hand of the nurse touched the arm of the child, when the nose was touched by a cotton swab, when he was put in a warm bath, or douched with water, and when a door was shut noisily.

Child 2:0;0 (+ 2) behaved in the same way when his covers were removed, when a plate was noisily dropped, when his eyes were washed, or when his foot was grasped suddenly.

Not before the age of one month does the child quiver and then cry when a light is suddenly switched on.

There are certain sensory stimuli which do not take effect through suddenness and strong intensity, but rather through the continuance of the causes. Among these are especially to be noted the effect of dampness, tight clothing or wrapping, wiping the child, and the contacts brought about by the visit of the physician. Crying can be observed as a result of tight or wet clothing in a whole series of cases, as early as the first month. Whether or not the wet is really the cause of the crying can be determined somewhat in the following way. If a child screams and is not quieted when a grownup lifts him or loosens his tight wrappings, but instead is quieted precisely in that moment when the wet covers are pushed away (which often is accomplished without a change of posture or any help from the grownup), then we can assert with some assurance that the wet was the cause of the crying. At the end of the second month, that child who kicks when permitted to lie uncovered cries if he is wrapped up.

In general, we can say that in the course of the first year sudden sensory stimuli suffer loss in effect. Shock reactions to stimuli, as we have described them, can be confirmed only in the first half year. The reaction to those stimuli which work through the duration of the stimulus is individually different.

(c) Abrupt and sudden changes of posture; uncomfortable posture. Sudden lifting up and rapid laying down often causes the child to cry. There are certain situations in which one can see that it is the change of position, as such, that is directly the cause of the crying. Such a situation occurs, for example, when the grownup firmly but gently, without any physical disturbance, changes the position of the child from lying down to sitting up. A similar situation occurs when a child, being lifted together with his crib, is pushed somewhat within his bed. Such crying can be observed even in the newborn child when the change of position is rough and abrupt if we can first eliminate with certainty the effect of the contact which is a concomitant in this situation. Beside these shock effects of a sudden change of position, it is important to take into consideration the effect of a continued, uncomfortable position. If the newborn is so placed that he lies with his face and stomach on his undercoverings, then he cries. Restriction of the freedom of movement, which occurs most of all when the child lies on his arms, increases the crying still more. In those situations in which the uncomfortable position is the cause of the crying, continued whimpering is characteristic. At the end of the first quarter year the effect of abrupt change of position already recedes into the background in the same way as did the influences of sudden sensory stimuli. And the uncomfortable position loses every meaning for that child who is able to change his position.

(d) Strong disturbances during sleep. The child often awakens with a cry. We are already aware of those cases in which sudden sensory stimuli, or the influence of continuous unpleasant stimuli, or the onset of pain can be recognized as the cause of the crying. But there are other cases in which the awakening crying can in no way be explained by the quality of the stimulus nor the method of its occurrence. Then the interruption of sleep, as such, seems to be the cause for crying. We have observed, for example, that a one month old child cries if he is awakened by the soft stroking of the mother, or by a nipple of a milk bottle being put very carefully between his lips. It seems in these cases that it is not the mother's stroking nor the nipple, which are ordinarily sources of pleasure and comfort to the child, but the fact that he is awakened, which causes him to cry.

(e) Fatigue. In the first days of life the child always falls asleep immediately after short periods of being awake. Later there are cases when one has the impression that the child is tired without being able to go to sleep. Then the child cries. No other cause for such crying is apparent except the fatigue itself, although the interpretation is still questionable. In these cases the child cries himself to sleep.

(f) Hunger. The child cries also from hunger—from the second or third day on. Although this crying issues from a displeasure-hunger, it is very likely that it must, nevertheless, to a certain extent, be considered as a cry of desire. This idea is to some extent confirmed by the movements which are associated with crying of this type. That is, at the end of the first month when the child cries, his crying is accompanied by sucking movements of the mouth. (Such movements usually occur only when an expected reaction is anticipated.) The characteristics of crying caused by hunger are: very loud, powerful screaming; accompanying movements; and quivering of all the soft parts of the mouth, the chin and the cheeks. After the first four months, crying begins not only when there is some direct unpleasant bodily contact, but it occurs also in those situations where some mental function is effective.

(g) Failure of the intended reaction. We have already said that the cry of hunger may contain a movement of longing. Crying of this type not only wards off the bodily discomfort of hunger, but—as shown by the suckling movements—it gives evidences of the anticipation of an expected satisfaction. One can therefore speak of a so-called "unsatisfied desire." The cry of unsatisfied desire can occur in situations other than those where hunger is the cause. It can probably also occur in those situations in which the child cries because his movements are inhibited. We have already said that restriction of the freedom of movement, such as a tight covering which hinders the kicking of the legs, or a tucking-in of the blankets so that the arms have no room to move, causes a child at the end of the first month to cry. Whether the child of this age cries because of the attempt to ward off these disturbing encroachments, or whether there is also a moment of desire—an expression of the longing to move freely—remains still to be discussed. When, however, the child is five months old, crying occurs clearly because of a failure of an intended movement. The first crying of this type is to be observed when the child fails to accomplish a movement that he tries to make—for example, if the child does not succeed in lifting his head when he tries to do so.

B 26:0; 5 sits upright quite high so that he is supported only with the hands, lies down again, raises himself once more, turns his head freely here and there, makes an attempt to move himself forward, but in spite of all efforts slips backward. Employs not only arms and legs in the effort of this forward movement, but the head as well. Again raises himself quite high in the prone position. He lays his head again on the under support, the periods of time during which he can hold up his head become constantly shorter. With a cry his head falls down for the last time. With discomfort he rolls and moves his head about on the undercover, accompanied by crying and restless movements. Again he supports himself on his arm, attempts even to hold himself supported on one arm only; his head again falls downwards. Once more he makes in vain the attempt to raise himself firmly on his arms. Crying begins anew.

From the beginning of the second month the striving toward the holding of a certain posture is often a cause of crying. Usually one body position—the one which the child has most recently mastered—is preferred above all others. A six months old child, whom we observed, cried as many times in the day as he was taken, for any reason at all, from the preferred prone position and laid on his back. A seven months old child cried if he was hindered, through his own fatigue or through the adult who straightened his position, from achieving a sitting position. The ten and eleven months old child who is able to stand, raises himself up again, crying if he is set or laid down.

The child's failure to grasp an object is the next cause of this type of crying. If a child's uncertain movements do not enable him to reach an object he begins, after several unsuccessful attempts, to make aimless, spasmodic movements and to cry.

G 28:0; 5 while in dorsal position in her bed turns her head towards the rear and makes grasping movements with her arms which are held high toward the glistening rods of the bed. The hands slide over the rods. She becomes restless, starts to kick about and, after several further unsuccessful attempts, begins to cry.

(h) Loss and removal of playthings. In the second half year the intention of the child extends itself towards objects. Then the child cries if anyone takes a toy away from him, or if he loses it. Before this time, say the fourth month, the loss of an object causes only a passing astonishment.

From the fifth month on, crying at the disappearance of a plaything is noted. Somewhat later the child begins to seek the lost plaything with searching glances, with grasping and groping movements. If his efforts are unsuccessful, the six months old child often begins to cry.

(i) Fear. Crying from fear begins clearly only in the eighth month. In our opinion, Watson has made a false conclusion if he means to take exception to the observation that fear is acquired so late. In our discussion we differentiate between fear and anxiety. We maintain that, in contrast to anxiety, which is physically founded, fear is psychically founded, and we maintain further that fear can occur for the first time only in that stage of development where a psychical moment can bring about an effect. According to our reasoning, therefore, it is conceivable that although Watson could produce shock reactions (frightened contractions) through strong bodily contacts, he produced as yet no fear reactions when he showed a child an animal. This is because the child was in that stage of development where these things—animals—do not mean a living thing at all, but instead mean only a kind of slipping-by impression of movements.

(j) Social influences. By social influences we mean all the impressions which go from any other human being directly toward the child. Such influences do not enter into the question as causes for crying in the first three months. The other person is for the child of this age significant, or is experienced by him only in relation to those manipulations which the child comes to know as proceeding from him. These manipulations— the being approached, the being wrapped up, the being put to bed—are the complexes of experiences together with which the child learns to know the grownup. These important life manipulations and the want of them are the first cause of affect or emotion. And so it happens that a child who is expecting a further manipulation, especially of feeding, cries not only when the grownup after several manipulations moves away from him, but even if he goes toward him. Were it true now, as it is later, that the approach of the grownup, as such, satisfies the child, then the child would not cry when the grownup comes closer. But in reality the person, as well as his speech, means nothing to him at this stage. The comforting manipulations with which the approach of people are associated have more positive effect.

With G 11 and B 12, both of the age of two months, we find exact proof that a person as such means as yet nothing. Both children cry when the grownup who wrapped them up leaves them or when they hear the human voice. As the mother bends over the bed of B 12, who looks quietly forward, the child begins to cry; and also G 11 cries if the sister stepping near her bed bends over her in order to dust it.

Only when the child is three to four months old— when his world extends outward from the immediate experiences of the body, when he begins to look about and to hear, when the world is experienced not only in direct immediate stimuli, but when the sounds and the gestures of the grownup (independent of those aforementioned manipulations) are understood—then only will the withdrawal of the adult out of the social-psychical adventure become for the child a cause for crying. The contact with other people, their speech, their play stimulations, have now a positive value, and the cessation of these contacts from now on is what causes the child to cry.[2]

So, for example, the five months old child increases his crying if a grownup enters the room but does not at once come to him. At nine months such crying may be caused by another circumstance—namely, if the grownup approaches another child.

G 45:0;9 begins once more to cry precisely in that moment when the nurse takes another child in her arms. Then G 45

[2] Concerning the genesis of this contact one can compare "approaching" in the first discussion in the volume, *Soliologische und psychologische Studien über das erste Lebensjahr.*

begins again to wander about in her bed. She begins to cry lustily as the nurse takes another child in her lap; she quiets herself again, however, squats down, and stands up again.

G 50:0; 10 babbles angrily twice at the observer, who takes another child in her arms and speaks to it.

A child of two months cries lustily if he hears another child who is crying. Here the strong, obtrusive, lasting stimulus produces, first of all, direct discomfort, and then displeasure connected his own crying sounds. These transfers of effect we have already discussed in detail, as the first step of social influence.

B 7:0; 1 opens his eyes and lies looking quietly about. The child in the next bed begins to cry and B 7 joins in the crying. B 7 opens his eyes and looks around. His neighbor begins to cry again and B 7 cries with him.

The newborn child from birth on utters short cries of fright and single sounds of displeasure—in addition to the monotone habitual crying. The newborn lets forth these short sounds of fright when affected by sudden strong sensory stimuli and by rough changes of position. Convulsive movements often take place at the same time. Contacts that are not very strong call forth single sounds of displeasure. B 1:0; 0 (+ 1) uttered sounds of this kind when his ears were cleaned. B 3:0; 0 (+ 9) made the same sound when his clothes were put on, when he was slowly laid down, and also, apparently, when he had a stomach ache that was not too severe. During sleep and quiet dozing, B 4:0; 0 (+ 6) gave forth single sounds of dissatisfaction if the covers which he had disturbed with his kicking were laid straight again.

In the second month the crying is no longer a monotone; instead, it varies in intensity, rhythm, and pauses.

As we have earlier remarked, hunger and pain cries can be definitely differentiated. We repeat the characteristics. The cry of pain is shrill, loud, and lasting, interrupted by whimpering and groaning, or it consists of short, single cries. The cry of hunger is loud, not lasting, varying in intensity, and interrupted by sucking movements. In uncomfortable positions the child whimpers.

We have already stated that crying in the first half year is always accompanied by movement. Very often, restless movements alone usher in the period of crying. Then come the single sounds which increase to crying. We see periods of movement alone alternating with periods of movement accompanied by sound utterances. Those movements which accompany and interrupt are just as important for the differentiation of the cause of the crying as are the sounds themselves. Observations on individual children confirmed what has just been said.

B 6:0; 1 is finished but not quite satisfied with his dinner. He lies there for a moment with his eyes open, closes his eyes, turns his head back and forth, opens his eyes again, sucks on the wrists of his left hand, which by a random movement of his hand accidentally came into contact with his lips, screams, presses his eyes together, moves his head and arms restlessly.

The cry of hunger is continuous, loud, and strong and is interrupted suddenly by suckling movements, even if an objective stimulus does not come into direct contact with the lips. During the time that suckling movements are being made, restless kicking and movements of the head temporarily discontinue, only to begin again with renewed vigor, accompanied by crying.

The Negatively Directed Reactions

B 12:0;2 has body pains. He cries shrilly and loudly, moves the head restlessly to and fro, explores with the hand restlessly and without aim over the face, opens the mouth wide, stretches the fingers, makes them into a fist, curves them, straightens them out; through flexing of the muscles he lifts his back from the crib, cries; the eyelids are pressed firmly together, the head travels to and fro restlessly, the arms are stretched out; the fists are clenched, moved toward the head, pushed out again; the head turns about to and fro; the legs kick vigorously to and fro; the tongue is stretched out and drawn back again. He remains silent for a moment. He begins again to get restless; the lips are moved, pursed, opened again; the mouth gapes; a low sound of discomfort is emitted, followed by shrill single sounds. With each shriek the eyelids are pressed firmly together. The single cries stop suddenly and he groans to himself and begins to whimper. The whimpering ceases and the movements become weaker. The eyes open and his glance rests on the bright window panes, after which the child quiets himself.

In the second month crying or shrieking becomes occasionally crying with tears. A kind of whimpering, and also, if the child is not too severely in pain, groaning and shrill single cries can be heard from this time on. In the two months old child one can now also observe the habitual crying, a crying which continues beyond an immediate need. Its characteristics are: uniformity, weakness, lack of variation in intensity, and interrupting pauses. The accompanying movements are also not very strong. Every excitement appears to be lacking in the child. The features show no expressional movements, neither positive nor negative; they exhibit also no attention to noise. This habitual crying differs from the single involuntary expelled sounds in that it is a continuous activity. In the ninth month the habitual crying of a second sort now begins. Either the child begins at once with the monotonous heedless vocalizations (this is more seldom by far), or he begins to cry for any reason whatsoever. He is uneasily astonished, experiences fear either from outer or inner stimuli, and begins to cry. Very soon the excitement abates, and only movement and vocalization persist.

G 0;2 begins to cry hard as soon as the nurse who was cutting her finger nails leaves her. After ninety-four seconds the crying becomes uniform and in monotone.

B 20:0;4. Strong crying becomes whimpering. After nine minutes the crying again increases and the movements which accompany the whimpering become livelier. Ninety seconds later the crying has become an even, unpausing, habitual crying. Eight minutes later the habitual crying with its movements ceases.

B 20 lies quietly looking around with wide-open eyes.

Whimpering, sighing, and sounds of groaning make their first appearance at the end of the second month. Sounds of displeasure that are constant can be found in individual children at the end of the fifth month. These sounds are not only different in tonefall and intensity, but they are phonetically different from other sounds, in much the same way as the constant sounds of surprise and joy, which can be observed at about the same time, are also different.

Thus, for example, G 30:0;6 began to use as a constant sound of displeasure *buh* and *erre erre;* G 51:0;10 when slightly displeased used *wua;* and G 54:0;11 when ill-humored said *awuwa.*

3. NEGATIVE EXPRESSIONAL MOVEMENTS. These enter the situation from the very first day of life on.

(a) In the frightened child we find a negative reaction of a more complex nature, one which is always accompanied by expressional movements. Then, when strong sensory stimuli are present, there follows a contraction or quivering of a reflex type, and often the utterance of a sound of fright also. In addition, crying and weeping often take place. To this behavior is sometimes added a whole series of expressional movements which, in the newborn, divide themselves principally into two forms. They are: first, crooking of the body, frowning of the forehead, straining of the legs, making fists, firm pressing together of the eyelids; and second, throwing back of the head, lifting up of the body, stretching out of arms, spreading of the fingers, opening the eyes wide.

A third somewhat milder form of fright can be observed in a one month old child if the sensory stimulus is not so strong. Quivering and trembling and sounds of terror are not present, but the eyes are opened very wide, the mouth opened, the eyebrows lifted, and the forehead wrinkled. Sounds of displeasure or crying accompany these movements.

(b) Several expressional movements of this third form are also to be observed in the case of surprise which, after all, is a kind of slight fright. They are to be considered as negative only if a negative sound is also uttered. In the first quarter year, these expressional movements of negative surprise, including the lifting of the arms, are usually the reaction to a sensory stimulus, change of position, or failure of the source of food, providing the hunger was already almost satisfied. Later, different events bring about these negative expressional movements. From the fourth or fifth month they occur at the failure to accomplish an intended movement, at the loss of a plaything, and when a social contact is discontinued.

(c) Until the fifth month the crying of a child is

always accompanied by movement. In the newborn we can already find expressional movements of displeasure without accompanying vocalization, although indeed less often than crying with accompanied movement. Besides the agitated aimless movements of the limbs and of the head which accompany the crying, the child, on the first day, contracts his face and presses his eyelids together tight. The one month old child wrinkles his forehead, squeezes his eyes together and weeps some large tears. The two months old child presses his lips firmly together, throws his head back, arches himself up, and flings the eyes open spasmodically, only to close them again.

(d) These expressional movements of active ill-humor have a different character from the expressional movements of passive displeasure, which is one of the forms of the condition of quiet waking. The signs of passive displeasure are: falling of the corners of the mouth, lack of luster in the eyes, and a puckering up of the nose. Quiet crying is to be observed all the while. Expressional movements of a passive displeasure do not appear before the seventh month. The seven months old child appears to have experienced the futility of the negative movements which accompany the utterances of active displeasure and to have given up their performance. Still, active and passive expressions of displeasure are not entirely detached. We find both in the seven months child without being able to associate each with its precise cause.

(e) These same expressional movements which occur with active and passive displeasure appear also with fear. We observed such movements in individual children of eight months of age. Take, for example, G 38:0; 8. If she was lifted out of her bed and carried out to the nursery while water was flowing into the bathtub, she simply endured it—that is, if no preparation for the bath was encountered, she remained on the arms of the nurse, laughing. Whereas B 42:0;8 and G 49:0;10 cried and displayed the expressional movements of active displeasure if they were lifted out of their beds in the presence of a physician. B 57:1;0 laid herself quietly down with an expression of passive displeasure when she encountered preparations for the change of a bandage of a severe wound which she had on the upper arm.

(f) We were able to observe temper and anger in only one case. G 48:0;9, with an angry cry, hit the nurse who dressed her and always kept laying her down again. As often as she raised herself, she kicked with her legs in great agitation. Hindered in her hitting, she displayed her temper by clenching her fists, pressing her lips together tightly, opening her eyes wide, and by wrinkling the forehead. The expressional movements of active displeasure appear here in increasing number. It is possible that the expressional movements of anger and temper are derived from active ill-humor, and the expressional movements of depression have their roots in the expressional movement of passive displeasure.

As concrete cases in which the described negative expressional movements could be observed, the following were chosen as examples:

1. Fright. B 50:0;1 trembles when the window is noisily shut. He moves his arms and legs about, clenches his fists, wrinkles his forehead, moves his fists toward his face and, after he has let out a low cry of fright, he begins to cry.

B 12:0;2 lies quietly gazing in his bed. An automobile goes by bumping over the street. He shrinks back and lets out a sound of fright, opens his eyes wide and throws his head back, stretches his arms sidewards, spreads his fingers, opens his mouth and utters a single cry of displeasure.

2. Negative Surprises. B 6:0;1. As the window is opened B 6 opens his mouth and eyes wide, stretches his arms sidewards, and utters sounds of displeasure.

G 11:0;2, who slumbers, becomes restless in her bed from the sound of the flowing water in her bathtub. She opens her eyes wide and then her mouth, turns her head, lifts her forehead a little, exhibits the typical expression of surprise, and begins to whimper.

3. Sounds of Active Displeasure. G 21:0;4 is evidently tired after lively play.

18.04[3] She is lying in her bed again, sucking on her thumb, and observing her fingers.

18.09 Yawns and begins to whimper.

18.11 Ceases whimpering, looks around, whimpers again, even-
18.12 tually begins vigorous shrieking. Quiets down, but as
18.14 soon as another child starts shrieking she, too, starts to scream.

18.18 Ceases screaming, plays with her hands, seizes the railings, pulls her ears, covers her face with her little hands.

18.20 Lifts her body and head; babbling, she throws off her covers.

18.28 Noticing the nurse, she starts to murmur. The murmur-
18.29 ing turns into loud screams. Covers her eyes with her
18.31 little hands, continues to scream, kicks with her little legs.

18.34 Quiets, turns her head sideways, closes her eyes, opens them again, turns her head to the other side, closes her eyes again, and tumbles down tired.

18.35 She is quiet. Now and then she opens her eyes.

18.40 Sleeps heavily and sound.

B 26:0;5, after being carried around in arms and returned

[3] The hours and minutes are given according to the Continental method, in which the hours from 1 P.M. to 12 midnight are represented by 13 to 24 o'clock inclusive.

to his bed, lies on his right side, weeping, his head pressed against the railing. The weeping turns into violent screaming, the accompanying light movements into trampling. He turns again on his back, kicking with his little arms and legs, blinking his eyes, turning his head restlessly, trembling with his entire body; moves violently and weeps piteously, blinks for a moment with eyes half open, stretches his arms high, rolls himself restlessly to and fro, clutches his hands, turns his head abruptly sideways, his fingers interlocked crampingly, stops for a moment, sticks his fingers into his mouth, pulls on them, opens his mouth, pulls them out abruptly and tries to suck his right fist. Tears run down from his eyes; he kicks the covers off and screams.

4. Sounds of passive displeasure. B 35:0;7 begins to cry when having his face washed—after an unsuccessful movement toward the hand of the nurse, quiets after an attack of hiccoughs, looks around quietly. The face muscles are lax, the eyes lusterless, the corners of his mouth sink. Only the nose is turned slightly upward.

G 45:0;9 who, due to loss of her playthings, started screaming, sits down quietly, rubbing her eyes with her little fists, blinking with lusterless eyes and frowning forehead.

B 52:0;10 who was separated from his playmate lies quiet, looking angrily at his bed. The eyes are dull and the corners of his mouth sink down.

According to their emotional content, the negative reactions are, in general, the expression of displeasure or negative influences; according to their meaning, they are either an inclination toward flight and defense, or they are an appeal to the helping activity of the member of the community in which the child is born. Finally, those negative reactions of displeasure are to be understood as movements having their origin in desire.

CHAPTER V

The Positive Reactions

1. Positively Directed Movements.

(a) Nourishment.[1] Jennings has already noted that the negatively directed reactions of an organism, in a primitive state, are far more numerous than the positively directed reactions. With few exceptions, the only mode of behavior which from the very beginning is surely positive is the taking of nourishment. The newborn makes suckling movements when his lips are touched, and the one month old child turns his head toward the source of food. The child makes suckling movements at the most varied opportunities, thus manifesting a positive turning toward the source of food even when the stimulation is insufficient. He, perhaps, thereby reveals the anticipation of a recalled, positive, well-liked act.

So we can accept the idea that, just as the events of anticipated desire arise from displeasure, so the turning toward reaction, occurring at the taking of food, is itself accompanied by pleasure. The expression of satisfaction immediately after the taking of nourishment also proves these facts. Of this we will speak later. The suckling movements play an important rôle in the movements included in the taking of nourishment inasmuch as the sucking is the first of the child's

[1] Nourishment will be discussed here from the viewpoint of positive reaction. A separate section is given to the remaining activities which accompany feeding. Compare Chapter VII.

movements which is purposeful and complete in bringing about a desired condition. As later, the various other series of movements are practiced as soon as the child has mastered them, are repeated under the name of function pleasure, and as play are displayed at all possible opportunities, so now, this one effective movement—this one movement which the newborn child can accomplish—becomes the chief activity of play. When the child is not hungry and, for any reason at all, an object is put between his lips, then the suckling movement is a diverted activity in much the same sense as other types of movements are, which we will see later. We have not seen fit to build up a mysticism out of this simple forerunner of play—as the Freudians attempt. We see in the suckling itself not a lust for pleasure, a desire within itself, but, according to Karl Bühler's conception, a function pleasure. The correctness of this assumption appears to be very precisely proved by the fact that a hungry, crying child can never be quieted by the mere opportunity to suck. Feeding means to him the real end desire, and pleasure concerned with the taking of food cannot be satisfied through the pleasure of mere suckling, because suckling is not a desire for pleasure. If one puts an object between the lips of a hungry child, he makes two or three suckling movements and then, all at once, throws out the object which does not bring him the awaited pleasure.

(b) Sensory stimulation and perception.[2] The positive reactions to the stimuli of perception are the most meaningful positively directed ways of behavior for the mental development of the human being. These are at the beginning, nevertheless, only sporadic and

[2] Compare with this presentation: Bühler K. *Die Geistige Entwiklung des Kindes,* section 7.

individual. In general we can say that strong sensory stimuli of any sort call forth negative reactions. At the very beginning, for example, the child seems to react sensitively to temperature. Cold is, in general, a negatively greeted stimulus. On the other hand, luke-warm and higher degrees of warmth are more or less pleasant, depending on the individual. Wet is, as we have earlier described, presumably quite as unpleasant as a harsh touch of a strong temperature stimulus. Every child likes to be wiped dry. We have, as a rule, not observed in the first three months positive reactions to even simple stimuli of contact. Most of these mentioned manipulations of the body of the child bring forth either direct displeasure or else are borne without any recognizable movement of expression. The expression of comfort is first observed only when a child is again made dry and laid in bed. Strong contacts connected with pain, and tickling, which later is pleasant and welcome, produce negative reactions. Only from the fourth month on, do stroking, blowing on the child, and tickling cause a positive reaction, and produce an expression of comfort. Not before the fifth month does the child laugh when he is touched. Changes of posture and the bodily movements going with it, belong quite as much to the earliest positive stimuli as the hindering of freedom of movement belongs to the negative. The mere change of position, nevertheless, is not thereby an outspoken positive stimulus. There are cases in which the child begins to exhibit positive expressional movements when he is merely being lifted up, laid down, and turned over. There are other cases, however, in which change of position produces reactions of fear and defense. The effect of the change of the position depends, moreover, somewhat on the situation. Freedom of movement and the movements of his body, however, always appear to give pleasure to the child (active and passive). He likes also to be moved to and fro, and to be shaken up and down. If a child is loosely bound he kicks with expression and pleasure, from the second month on. We have already shown that the restriction of freedom of movement is received negatively by the one month old child.

On the whole, acoustical and optical stimuli of a slight or limited intensity remain unobserved during the first and second months. Occasionally it will be noted that the child turns toward light and toward the source sound. In general, babies become aware only of very strong and very sudden stimuli—observation in the negative sense. Only when the child is two or three months old does he turn repeatedly toward a lighted spot. It is the same with the beginning of active listening and touching. Now at the age of two or three months, the child turns his head with regularity toward the source of the sound while the sound lasts. He touches what is hidden under his hand, his mouth, his lips, and, somewhat later, he follows a moving object with his glance. With this behavior we are permitted to see the first physical signs of attention and interest —namely, straining of the features of the face, slight wrinkling the forehead, pursing the lips, sticking out the tongue, tightening the muscles of the eyes, and impulsive noises which interrupt the movements during the act of perception. It was often observed in a two months old child that, while he was staring toward a certain point with all the characteristics described above, suddenly the signs of attention disappeared, and at the same time his eyes began to squint. This staring at a single spot is one of the most beloved occupations of a three months old child. In the case of B 12, who was observed by us during the second and third months of his life, the progress in this direction could be precisely established. It can be said that in the case of the two months old B 12 the expressional movements, described above, occurred only twice in the course of the day, but we observed signs of attention ten times. Of these, eight times the interest was reflected in the face.

The child of three months turns his head toward the source of the stimulus not only while the sound continues but often after the sound ceases.[3]

The child of four months continues to glance in the direction in which an object was moving, but from which it has been withdrawn. That means that the progress of the positive reactions is similar to that which obtained with the negative reactions—that after the first quarter year, stimuli outside of those of immediate bodily contact become effective, and are actively seen and actively heard.

B 16:0; 3 turns his head in the direction of sound caused by flowing water in a bath tub. Just in the moment in which the water was turned off, the stimulus also ceased its influence.

B 21:0; 4 follows with his eyes the rattle which by accidental movements of his hands was shaken up and down. The eyes blinked always just a few seconds afterwards in the direction in which they followed the rattle, even if the rattle was then sounded on the other side.

Only from the third month on does the child make positive movements toward sensory stimuli with two

[3] This criterion for active listening was established by us in the same way as the earliest reaction to the human voice.

organs at the same time. It must therefore be generally accepted that previously the child responded actively in only one direction, so to speak, and accordingly responded only to a single condition, or experience.

Out of these exact observations are yielded certain deductions which Koffka constructs into a most highly improbable hypothesis based not at all (in our opinion) on the foregoing observations. Koffka explains, "We cannot state, moreover, that the child sees a lighted spot, but that on a relatively even ground the child sees a lighted spot. He explores the encroachment with his hand which up till then lay there disregarded, in one place. To sum up briefly:

"From that undefined and uncertain ground there arises a definite and more certain phenomenon—a quality with which the facts of the structural ability of the world of perception of the newborn shall be demonstrated. Were it really so, in the case of turning toward the light and sound, for example, that the impression arises from a 'relatively even ground,' then the relatively even ground must be present before the appearance of the sensory perception. This would mean that, up to a certain degree, the entire world of perceptions is present to the child . . . as is the case with the adult."

This concept we shall not even discuss. We consider it much more likely that the newborn is completely shut in within himself, and that only a very strong stimulus forces a new experience on him. Koffka's hypothesis constructs the consciousness of the newborn after the pattern of a fully developed consciousness which lives, well established in all directions, completely on the qui vive, and already oriented toward impressions of all sorts. The idea that the newborn makes any active forward turning reaction without the force of a strong stimulus does not even enter the question—so far as we see it. Our exact observations show that the newborn child's state of waking, as indicated by the failure of all inner and outer stimuli, is a kind of semi-consciousness as the "ground" out of which the sensory impression projects itself. Then there is theoretically nothing to be said against it. Only, the structural postulations of Koffka contain much more. They maintain, for example, that each impression of light must arise from a previously undifferentiated optical background, and this is an opinion without support in practice. In this condition of semi-consciousness the child lacks every consciousness of the surrounding world, and only through strong stimuli is he snatched out of slumbering and jostled into an activity of sensory organs.

How slowly and by what progressive connecting steps the transition from one reaction to another sort is accomplished can be further observed. We will give several examples which show an already advanced stage of development—that is, which show threads connecting the reactional transition. The child is two months old before he first begins to listen to his own vocalizations and to repeat single sounds which he has uttered and heard. The child is three months old before he first seeks the source of the sound with his eyes, and now adds eye movements to the restless head movements which occur during the continuance of the noise. Only when the child is four months old does he gaze toward his hands when they touch an object. Then the organs of speech, and the sense of hearing, the sense of sight, and that of touch begin in these cases to coördinate—to work together.

single finger, putting the thumb opposite to the other finger. Grasping with one hand is after all possible only through this opposite placement. As an intermediate step there is to be noted the time when the child, using one hand, does not use the fist, but instead the palm of the hand in grasping. The fingers and also the fists are then still spasmodically outstretched.

At the beginning of the second half year the child is no longer satisfied to reach only toward those objects which are in his immediate neighborhood. It is characteristic of this age that children actually grasp toward all objects which they see. Now bodily posture is also put into the service of the grasping; the child turns himself toward things, and the body enters the grasping situation as a third component. In the second half year we rarely find any further attempt of the child to assist the grasping movements of the hand by accompanying movements of the mouth, or of the head. Between the sixth and ninth months the legs are used to assist in grasping. In much the same way as the first primitive grasping of the hands, the object is now taken between the soles of the feet. Legs and hands alternate with each other in this newly developing grasping play till in the last quarter of the year the legs come to have their own occupation and become useful in the change of posture, in moving forward, and take no further part in the grasping play.

While B 23:0;3 is being undressed he lays hold of his shirt on which his hands had traveled to and fro, and then he lifts and lowers it.

G 21:0;4 is shown the rattle. She lifts both hands toward it and, as she moves her balled fists toward each other, succeeds in really reaching the rattle.

The rattle is shown to her again. Her aimless movements with which, from right to left, she approaches one hand to the rattle made it possible to push the rattle out of the hand of the nurse so that it fell down.

G 21 is stimulated to grasping movements by the presentation of a rattle. She moves it about first aimlessly and restlessly with both arms in the air. Then she stretches the arms sidewards, lifts them up, moves the fists near to each other, but also reaches toward the rattle. This grasping is repeated innumerable times. She lifts the fists up, moves them near to each other, but also reaches toward the rattle. This grasping is repeated innumerable times. She lifts her head out of the dorsal position and seeks to reach the rattle with her mouth.

B 20:0;4 observes attentively the rattle which his mother holds towards him, sticks out his tongue, and stretches out his fists towards her.

B 26:0;5 grasps toward bed railings with both hands. The fingers are spread apart, the thumb is already placed opposite the other fingers.

Only at the fourth and fifth months is independence from the direct effect of the stimulus reached in grasping, and, at the same time, the coördination of seeing and grasping is established. Now the child reaches toward an object which is not in his immediate neighborhood, but is merely seen by him. We can follow all the steps of the child's progress, from the first grasping of that which is nearest to him, to constant active conquering behavior wherein he always grasps.

If one observes the behavior of a child who is first sitting straight up and then, spying an object near by, stretches his arms in jerky fashion, one will see (in spite of the fashionable condemnation of automatism and mechanism) that it resembles the performances of a doll to which life had been given, so to speak, limb after limb. This painstaking coördination of the reactive complexes of movement is, however, to be completely differentiated from the active "life unfolding" of the impulsively self-moving child. The spontaneous activity of the "unfolding" limbs is completely other than the reactive behavior. More of that later!

(d) Social approach. This research confirms the conclusions set forth in a previous publication—namely, that the child is positively directed toward other human beings. The first social approach occurs in the second month. While the one month old child observes other people just as little as other objects, and reacts to the auditory stimulus of the human voice by sucking, as though it were a stimulus accompanying the occurrence of food, in the second month the glance of the child allows itself to be enticed by the glance of the grownup. At this time one can observe a slight quiver of genuine smiling in response to the voice and glance of the human being. In this there is conceived, somehow, at least the foregoing stage of a specific reaction to the human being, as such. The smiling reactions, as well as all other reactions toward the human being in the first year of life, are a positive turning toward him—the returning of the glance, the seeking of the glance, turning of the head and body toward the person, stretching out of the hands, babbling, catching a glance and therefore neglecting the toy, attempting to rouse attention through movements, offering him an object—turning toward him when frightened or surprised.

An anti-social behavior, that is, a behavior negatively directed toward presence of people, does not occur in the first year of life, but does very clearly in the second.

Social reaction to playmates of the same age takes place later than to adults. Only at the age of five months is another child perceived, observed with attention, and, when the glance of both perchance meet, smiled at. These reactions remain the only reactions observed by us until the child is nine months old. It

TABLE III *

The Observed Reactions of Children Toward Grownups

Age in months	1 2 3 4 5 6 7 8 9 10 11 12
Returns the glance of the adult with smiling ..	
Is quieted by touching....................	
Becomes restless by being spoken to........	
Cries when the grownup who was attending him, leaves.................................	
Smiles back at grownup...................	
Disturbed when approached...............	
Returns approaching glance with lalling......	
Displeasure when the child loses the glance of the grownup...........................	
Quieted by caressing......................	
Disturbed by the sight of people...........	
Neglect of play through meeting the glance of the grownup...........................	
Striving for attention by lalling............	
Stretches out hands towards the grownups....	
Cries when the grownup stops talking........	
Strives for attention by movements.........	
Pulls on the clothes of the grownup.........	
Offers the grownup an object..............	
Imitates the movements of the grownup with a plaything.............................	
Organized play activity...................	
Looks at grownup amazed because of an incident.................................	

* This and the following tables contain only those reactions which could be established in at least 60 per cent of the observed children.

must be especially noted, however, that the children in our case were not deliberately brought into situations which forced a social contact and were separated one from the other by a considerable distance. Every child was confined to his bed, which rendered the achievement of a social contact even more difficult. At nine months the child lalls to the other child, offers him playthings, and cries bitterly if the grownup gives his attention to another child. The nine months old child still permits toys to be taken quietly out of his hand when a playmate grasps them. The ten months old

TABLE IV

The Observed Reactions of One Child Toward Another

Age in months	1	2	3	4	5	6	7	8	9	10	11	12
Observes other child												
Smiles at other child												
Cries if the other child receives attention												
Offers toy to other child												
Lalls to other child												
Imitates the movements of another child												
Opposes toy being taken away												
Organized play activity												
Strives for attention by means of lalling												
Ill-humor, if another child moves away												
Setting aside toy and turning toward a child												

child already opposes the toy being taken away. The eleven months old child concerns himself with gaining the attention of another child by lalling. He shows displeasure when the child moves away. With the eleven months old child we find organized play activities. The eleven months old child throws a plaything away in order to grasp toward the comrade who is in this way brought nearer, a behavior which is similar to the five months old child who plays only so long as the adult is not present, or else he forgets his play in order to observe him.

Our individual observations in this field bring both Tables III and V together.

Table V shows the increase of the frequency of social relations in general, and the percentage part of the single age-levels in the sum of all observed social reactions.

TABLE V

Percentual Relation of the Individual Age-levels to the Whole Sum of Social Reactions

Age..........	0;1	0;2	0;3— 0;4	0;5— 0;6	0;7— 0;8	0;9— 0;10	0;11 1;0	Total
Relation of the individual age-levels to the whole sum of social reactions in %...	0	5	12	13	19	26	25	100

CHILD AND GROWNUP (an example)

G 21:0;4 returns the glance of the nurse who looks at her, with laughing and cooing.

G 30:0;6 turns herself around from back to stomach and seeks to draw the attention of her grandmother toward herself by lalling.

G 31:0;6 clasps the bottle with hands while drinking. Through a clumsy movement the bottle falls. She lalls loudly to the nurse.

B 50:0;10 seizes the coat of the doctor, pulls on it, coos, beats on the doctor's shoulder after raising himself in his bed, amuses himself by shaking to and fro, holding on to the bedstead. When the doctor still continues to turn her back, he walks up and down in his little bed, laughing and lalling, clicks his tongue, tugs again at the coat hanging down behind the bedstead.

G 51:0;10 looks at the observer who is deep at work writing, scratches with her nail on the cover, makes a noise with a rattle, in the meanwhile looking carefully and continually at the observer.

At the age of nine months the child shows objects to the grownup. The grownup's movements with a plaything are imitated, and the child at the age of one year who is either surprised or frightened seeks to meet the glance of the grownup. The child appears to ask the adult, "Do you see it also?" In the grasping and offering of objects there lies the beginning of an organized, social play activity with the grownups.

B 50: 0; 10 holds his doll out toward the observer, allows her to take the doll from him, and laughs as it is returned to him. Holds it out again.

G 51: 0; 10. The nurse picks up the doll which had fallen down. The nurse presses the doll, which squeaks, and gives it to the child again. She holds it, then gives it back again. Finally she keeps the doll and seeks to produce a tone by pressing as the nurse had done. As it is accomplished she is very pleased.

CHILD AND CHILD

G 28: 0; 5 glances always toward the other child who lies in her crib about one yard away.

G 26: 0; 5 looks at a child who sits on the swaddling table which stands at the foot of her bed. Accidentally the eyes of both children meet in a glance, and they both laugh.

B 50: 0; 10 looks attentively at G 44, offers her again the rattle. G 44 takes it back again, holds it out again—and so on.

Here is described in detail a scene which took place between B 53: 0; 10 and B 73: 0; 11 while they were being observed.

B 53 drums lustily on the night table. His neighbor B 73 stands up opposite him in his crib and beats on the railing of his crib with "da da," which B 53 always immediately imitates.

B 53 turns himself about for a moment. As he again spies B 73, who again makes a movement before him, B 53 ceases to play with the coverlet, sits and rocks with his entire body as B 73 did before. Both children look at each other, laugh and gurgle. Then B 53 stands up and wanders around in his bed. Finally he grabs a pillow, lifts it up, lets it fall, sits down, pulls on the bands with which he is fastened, lalls in a lively manner and winks at B 73 who looks at him from the neighboring bed. B 73 now seeks the attention of B 53, who is deep in his play with the pillow, and makes movements in his bed—to no purpose. Finally he walks up and down in his bed, whimpers on and off uneasily, sits down again, pulls the coverlet off and on, crawls here and there, kneels in front of the bed slats, stands up again, rocks to and fro and keeps on doing so until B 53 looks at him. Then they both laugh. B 73 stretches his arms through the slats in the railing, sits down, stands up, seizes the cover, lalls to B 53, until finally B 53 turns away and walks up and down in his own bed.

(e) Overcoming negative reactions. So long as the child still reacts to all strong sensory stimuli it is possible to distract the child who is ill-humored. For those same sense stimuli which in the first quarter year of life call forth the negative reactions can also cause them to stop. Rapid change of position, touching, and sight and sound stimuli are very effective for this purpose. Distraction through means of acoustical stimuli seldom takes place after the passing of the first quarter year. From then on new influences, those which are brought about through people, enter the situation as the means of pacifying. The fixed glance of the adult, his attention to the child, can bring about quietude. From the fifth month on, an object which is given into the hand of the child to play with can also pacify him. In all cases the diverting comes about through stimuli which thrust themselves in from the outside. We have observed that from the sixth month on the child is no longer so completely absorbed in negative reactions as in the foregoing months. He discovers for himself an object which he draws near in grasping play or he busies himself with a sensory stimulus which is not too strong. This fact gives evidence of the development of active interest and of the retreat of the negative reaction as the "dominant" in behavior. From this time on we see negative reactions occurring more and more often, only as accessory reactions.

We present the following observations:

B 4 : 0 ; 0 (+ 10) cries. He is lifted up, quieted, is laid again in his crib, begins in a short while to cry again.

B 4 begins to cry. He is taken out, quieted, lies quietly with his eyes open, begins to cry, however, as soon as he is laid in his crib.

B 71 : 0 ; 0 (+ 5) lies in his crib on a large sheet. He begins to cry. The observer lifted high the sheet on which he lay and B 71 stopped.

B 5 : 0 ; 1 cries and moves himself restlessly. The observer speaks to the child very loudly from her place by the window. Immediately he ceases as long as the sounds continue. Cries when he is undressed, but being put in the bath quiets him.

B 13 : 0 ; 2 cries vigorously. The shower is turned on. The sound of the flowing water causes him to stop.

B 12 : 0 ; 2 is displeased, moves himself restlessly and cries. A child in the room begins to cry. He stops.

B 23 : 0 ; 4 stops crying suddenly in order to follow with his eyes a nurse who is going by.

G 25 : 0 ; 4 begins to cry and to move herself restlessly. Suddenly her glance rests on her own hands. She interrupts her crying and follows the hands with her eyes.

B 38 : 0 ; 7 begins to whimper. Then he busies himself again, takes a rubber doll, presses it when it squeaks. He sticks it in his mouth, and pulls it out again.

G 45 : 0 ; 9 walks along the railing of the bed crying.

B: 1 ; 0 begins cryingly to play with his doll. He is, in fact, because of it, quiet for a moment.

B: 0 ; 9 sits in his go-cart. He cries; if one speaks to him he is still.

B: 1 ; 0 stands in his bed, looks about attentively in the other room and cries loudly all the while. Suddenly he sits down and plays with his little dress.

2. POSITIVE EXPRESSIONAL MOVEMENTS.

(a) We have already stated that the positive expressional movements are more scarce and occur later than the negative. During the first month of life expressional movements of a positive sort are to be observed, but only in a very limited field—that of taking nourishment. Thirsty, hasty drinking, hardly interrupted for breathing, appears to give positive enjoyment. This may be a kind of function pleasure. More of this later.

(b) Bodily comfort. At the end of the first month the child displays a well-defined expression of comfort when he has had enough to eat, when being bathed, if he has slept thoroughly, and if he is dry and warm and in a comfortable position. This positive expression of comfort has somewhat the following characteristics: glowing eyes, mouth lifted at the corners, and a slow closing of the mouth. The muscles of the face are firmer than in the state of passive dozing. There is lacking, however, the straining which goes with other forms of quiet waking as, for example, when the child gives attention to something.

9.20   As B 12:0;2 is laid in his bed after being fed, he yawns and stretches himself.

9.23   Rubs his eyes with his fists. He lies quietly there gazing.

9.26   He appears satisfied and as having had enough to eat;

the eyes gleam, the corners of the mouth are turned up just a little. He stretches his arm out once again. Falls asleep.

B 50:0; 1 is laid in his bed after a warm bath. He lies quietly there with open mouth; the corners of his mouth are turned up, the eyes slightly shining.

In the second month this type of expression develops into laughing. At the beginning it is perhaps reflective; at any rate, it occurs then only as a specific expressional movement of social meaning. The glance and voice of human beings are what first cause the child to smile. The situations in which smiling occur are shown in the following table.

Table VI

Causes of Childish Laughter

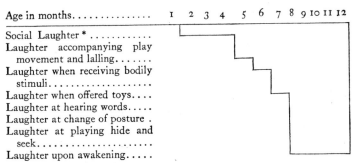

Age in months..............	1	2	3	4	5	6	7	8	9	10	11	12
Social Laughter *...........												
Laughter accompanying play movement and lalling.......												
Laughter when receiving bodily stimuli.................												
Laughter when offered toys....												
Laughter at hearing words.....												
Laughter at change of posture .												
Laughter at playing hide and seek..................												
Laughter upon awakening.....												

* By social laughter is here indicated that which occurs when the child sees or hears another person.

From this it can be seen that smiling at the beginning is specifically and exclusively a social function, and that only later it happens in connection with experiences other than just the hearing and seeing of people.

TABLE VII

The Relation Between Smiling in the Social Situation and
Smiling as a General Reaction (in per cent)

Age	Social laughter in response to		Total	Laughing as a general reaction	Total
	The Grownup	The Child			
0 ; 1	—	—	—	—	—
0 ; 2	100	—	100	—	100
0 ; 3	89	—	89	11	100
0 ; 4	92	—	92	8	100
0 ; 5	60	15	75	25	100
0 ; 6	50	—	50	50	100
0 ; 7	49	13	62	38	100
0 ; 8	20	30	50	50	100
0 ; 9	10	40	50	50	100
0 ; 10	40	30	70	30	100
0 ; 11	25	50	75	25	100
1 ; 0	10	40	50	50	100

(c) Function pleasure. As function pleasure Karl
Bühler has designated those pleasures which can accompany the organized course of a certain succession
of movements, as well while they are being practiced
as when they have been mastered. There is a stage of
function pleasure which seems to precede that of the
organized movements. In a certain stage, before the
child practices and enjoys specific successions of movements, he seems to enjoy and to give himself over to
bodily movements and vocalizations which become always more organized and rhythmic. In the case also
of certain stimuli of perception one has the impression
that the child is positively attuned—staring at them
and listening to them. The first signs of such function
pleasure are lifting of the corners of the mouth, and
gleaming of the eyes. All these bodily movements and

series of perceptions which are constantly repeated and attended by positive expressional movement are to be already considered as the beginning of play. These ever more specific movements and later the manipulation of objects, of which there is still much to be said, take place generally with a positive attitude of the practicing, playing child, and with expressional movement of pleasure. Expressional mimicry movements of a new sort hardly enter the situation.

(d) Interest. While in the first two months, only a strong direct influence on the child brings about a reaction of interest, from then on the child, to a certain extent, is in a state of passive receptivity, of readiness, conditioned to receive impressions to which he is disposed. One can see the expressional movements of interest—the opening wide of the mouth, tensing of the muscles of the face, slight wrinkling of the forehead, pursing of the mouth, and stretching out the tongue. In the second half year there can be seen, in addition to these, prolonged stretching of the body, stiffening of the muscles, and a slight leaning toward an object of interest. In the second month there is also a condition of being awake which is quiet and receptive, a condition in which the child does not move himself, but which does not appear to be the same or as complicated as dozing. Of semi-consciousness or dozing we will speak at length later. This state of quiet waking does not appear to be one of only quiet comfort, but seems rather to be a state in which the child receives impressions of the surrounding world.

In the readiness to reception lie those beginnings which one can later designate as interest, and which one can find in active accomplishment. It is difficult to assert exactly when interest occurs as an active mental approach. Aside from the already mentioned expressional movements of mimicry there occur in the second year of life approach movements of the whole body, which perhaps only now permit one to speak of an active interest.

From the seventh month on we find several expressional movements of the receptive condition in cases in which the gathered data speak against a mere reciprocal reception of perceptions. A tightening of the features of the face, a pursing of the lips, a tension of the body—these, it is true, reveal attention. The eyelids, however, are lightly pressed together and the influence of the expression of the face is eliminated. The child, as it were, appears to be inwardly listening and to be busy with his inner self. Since we cannot differentiate what the child perceives in himself, then we dare not presume the beginning of a sort of mental activity in this contemplative condition of wakefulness.

We repeat again the characteristics of the different waking states:

1. Quiet dozing [6]—sleepy facial expression, absence of any gleam in the eyes.

2. State of comfort—uplifting of the corners of the mouth, faint wrinkling of forehead, shining eyes, slow opening of the eyes.

3. State of receptive waking—tightening of the features of the face, faint wrinkling of forehead, eyes wide open, pushing forward of the lips, pursing of the mouth.

4. State of passive displeasure—dull eyes, sinking of the corners of the mouth, rumpling of the nose.

[6] Dozing is used throughout as a translation of the German "Dämmerzustand" which means literally, "condition or state of twilight." An adequate idea of the condition intended by the word "dozing" can be obtained from the text.

The Positive Reactions

5. State of contemplative waking—tensing the features of the face, faint wrinkling of the forehead, eyelids lightly pressed together, pushing forward of the lips, pursing of the mouth.

In the second half year, as we have already seen, the child directs his grasping movements toward objects which are not in his immediate neighborhood but which capture his attention. His eyes dwell attentively and for a long time on objects which do not seem unusually worthy of attention, which neither through gleam or color or movements separate themselves from the surroundings. The eyes, which until then wander about from one object to another, light upon one object accidentally and remain there. They appear to want to receive new perceptions through the searching activity with objects. These facts—the condition of contemplative wakefulness, the new expressional movements of interest, the awakened active attention to his inner world—permit us here to assume the beginning of active interest. To a certain extent the child himself now seeks stimuli.

(e) Positive surprise. Positive surprise enters later than negative surprise and then in three different forms. From the third month on come the well-known expressions of surprise—opening wide of the eyes and of the mouth, stiffening of the muscles of the forehead, sideward stretching of the arms, often brought about through a pressing interest. We can speak, then, of an interested surprise. This can be observed when the child, experiencing strange sensations, is impressed by new sensory stimuli which are neither too strong nor too unpleasant. Joyful expressional movements of surprise followed by signs of pleasure were already observed in a five months old child when a plaything, which had been hanging over his crib and was removed from his view, was again placed within his glance, or if the adult who passed by the child again approached him. We found that the eight months old child exhibited joyful surprise at the return of an adult to whom he was accustomed if the adult had been absent for some time—say over night. It seems that a strange or new impression brings about an interested surprise, and a recognition brings about a joyful surprise. In addition to these two forms of surprise we found the expressional movements of surprise occurring without their being followed by either interest or joy. This movement consists of a short turning toward anything, and it is usually caused by the disappearance of a plaything.

Expressional movements of positive surprise which give evidence that the child anticipates a state of satisfaction can be observed at eight months of age. When the child has reached this development, preparations for feeding do not produce negative reactions. On the other hand, however, neither do they release any vigorous reactions of desire. The child merely appears confident that he awaits fulfillment. The signs of this expectation are a certain tension of the features of the face, and the kind of posture the body assumes. Otherwise there is complete quiet. From the ninth month on preparations for bed or dressing for the daily walk also invoke expressional movements of the kind just described.

(f) Joy. It is the stimulation received through the senses and the comfort derived from a good organic condition that bring about the first positive expressional movements. Not until the second half year can one say that these positive expressional movements are out-wardly and objectively directed.

At the end of the fifth month we find, in addition to that comfort due to bodily well-being, a definite positive condition of comfort and, in addition to those expressional movements brought about by sensory stimuli, we find a whole series of newer, more positive expressional movements of which we can speak collectively as expressional movements of joy. The following movements can be observed: aimless movements of the arms and legs, vigorous turning of the head and hitting of the child's own shoulder, lifting up the corners of the. mouth, blinking of the eyes, lively opening and closing of the mouth. In the sixth month joyful clapping of the hands and laughing take place as general reactions. The *sounds* of happiness, still to be described, are just as numerous. In addition to the glance of the human being, funny movements or the repetition of the funny sound first cause outbursts of joy. Already at the age of five months, a child rejoices and shakes himself in a satisfied manner if he raises himself, alone, out of the prone position and supports himself on his hands; or if a group of sounds seems especially comical to him. All newly achieved positions of the body, such as sitting, standing, going forward, sideward turning, crawling, walking, as well as the assistance of grownups in cases of impossible achievement, bring forth such sounds of joy. Somewhat later the child makes aimless movements in a happy manner if he succeeds in reaching an object for which he was striving with his hands. Following moving objects with his eyes and joyful surprise cause a five months old child to give forth sounds of pleasure. At seven months of age the child first displays pleasure when a plaything is put in his hand. He also manifests his pleasure very vigorously during the pauses when he is eating something he likes very much—such as sweet apple compote. The eight months old child greets the food which is offered him with joy, and makes certain sounds which the grownup repeats. Certain games, such as hide and seek and similar games, at this time already give the child pleasure. In the second half year the joyful outbreaks become more frequent and of longer duration, and the condition of quiet comfort is continuously lessened.

(g) Desire. We have already dealt with desire in connection with those negative reactions which, we thought, contained a moment of desire. We can definitely state that at five months of age there occur positive expressional movements of desire which are, in part, accompanied by other expressional movements. Such movements are a demanding outstretching of the hands, and an anxious look toward the desired object. Such a look is often accompanied by demanding sounds.

3. Positive Vocalizations.

Karl Bühler has differentiated three functions in human speech: the expression, the call for help, and representation. While the expressions of feeling and call for aid can be observed in the vocalization of animals, the use of speech as representation appears to be primarily specifically human. Even the human child of the first year of life does not use vocalization as a means of representing things. His first vocalizations are extended expressional movements—therefore sounds of expression. The first crying is not an *intended* call for help, but rather in a biological sense is presumably to be considered just as objective as the cry of animals. The first child sounds are also positive expressional movements—that means that the positive expressional movements indicate a state of comfort. They issue directly from a waking condition of quiet comfort. Individual sounds and whole series of sounds are to be noted throughout the first year as expressions of comfort, and then later as expressions of pleasure and joy.

The one month old child utters single sounds when he is in a quiet condition of comfort, the two months old child utters sounds of pleasure to accompany his movements. The three months old child utters sounds of a positive nature when perceiving sensory sensations. The six months old child already crows happily; the seven months old child makes shouts of joy, clicks his tongue and squeaks, and, in addition to these three vocalizations, he lets loose a prolonged cry of satisfaction.

As the child comes into further contact with his surroundings he adds to these pure functional utterances expressions of emotion. These are the first vocalizations which release an intentional sound. The child looks at the grownup and seems to say, "See how happy I am."

Something new now occurs—something which points the way to the later use of speech as an implement of imparting facts (representation). The new use of vocalization has its roots in one of the individual sounds of different phonetic sounds which occur through the lalling of the two months old child. We can establish the difference between this kind of utterance and expressional movements by exact criteria. It is this: that whereas the sounds of expressions are uttered unnoticed and without an effort of will, the sounds of lalling are produced with directed attention—indeed, later they are deliberate and are continued as an activity. Function pleasure seems to accompany this lalling in much the same way as it accompanied the already mentioned practice of many series of movements. With a sort of effort the child is so completely given over to the lalling, that he discontinues all other activities as soon as he begins this one. He seems deliberately to practice funny sounds. So the lalling of the two months old child is accompanied only by impulsive movements, and only when the child is three months old is lalling accompanied by playful movements—movements which make necessary the attention of the child. At even an earlier stage, the child appears intentionally to repeat groups of sounds, listening the while to his self-produced vocalizations.

Next there is established a definite constancy of the coördination of certain sounds in certain conditions. This arises probably through the repetition of "giving expression." By the end of the first year this coördination of certain sounds is further developed and established by the child through his imitations of the more coördinated sounds of the grownup. In this way G 51:0; 10 uses "da da" when she becomes aware of an adult or a milk bottle, and B 50:0; 10 says "da da" when he stretches out his hands toward persons going by, or toward a piece of paper on the night table. G 54:0; 11 uses a demanding "wawawa." The preferred words of our twelve months old children are baba, dada, wawa, nana, mamam; they are developed through repetition.

In the same way as the negative reactions are the expressions of displeasure and of negative emotion, so the positive reactions are likewise the expression of pleasure and positive emotions. In the newborn the positive expressions are far less important than the negative. Since, however, they finally supersede the negative reactions in importance even during the first year of life, they will be treated again later.

CHAPTER VI

The Spontaneous Reactions

CHARACTERISTIC, uncoördinated, and purposeless movements have been observed in the infant as early as Preyer. By purposeless and uncoördinated we mean those movements which, from the first day of life on, are brought about by the individual separate movements of all the limbs of the body occurring, as they do, in motley confusion, in inimitable array, and in an unrepeatable succession. These movements are not at all purposeful, they do not strive toward a goal, nor do they receive attention on the part of the child. We can speak of the newborn child in the same way as we do of the protozoa—that he is in constant movement unless he is sleeping or in the state of dozing yet to be described. And truly all his movements in the first and second months of life, except the direct purposeful ones (such as the taking of nourishment, crying when hurt bodily, flight and turning away movements when receiving sensory stimulation), are such impulsive movements. They appear to be the direct outlet of an unfolding, pressing activity with which the living being is born. They are a condition of the system itself and are in no way happenings in response to an outer stimulus. They are neither positive nor negative, nor are there any sort of symbols which one could describe as expressional movements. Neither does functional pleasure seem to accompany them. They disappear proportionately in that degree in which attentive activity with the child's own body or playthings begins, but they keep their existence in a form of floundering and careless playful movements which are to be found even in grownups.

The activities and the performances which are brought about through these impulsive movements are in a certain sense opposite to the simple positive or negative reactions. The positive and negative reactions we have characterized throughout as either a turning toward or a turning away from a certain stimulus—an acceptance of the approaching stimulus or else a rejection through flight and defense. For the activities and performances which have the character of impulsive movements the positive approach, through which there are differences to be distinguished from the impulsive movements, is not the goal; but the activity proceeds freely out of this approach. In the case of simple positive or negative reactions we note the following. For example: a strong optical stimulus meets the eyes of the child. He turns his head away and the performance is ended. Another optical stimulus meets the eyes and he turns toward it and that performance is ended. Should, however, the impulsive movements of activities begin without a stimulus just then having encountered his eyes, then the child's glance travels here and there and seeks the stimulus. The movement is positively directed in the sense previously characterized—that the child turns himself toward the stimulus. The activity has, perhaps, also an accent of pleasure. But from here on a lively activity unfolds itself in these performances, different from those reactions which result only from a stimulus—a lively activity which appears to seek a field of practice. As in the case of the impulsive movements, these activities of the living organism exhibit themselves as completely aimless, and as though merely meeting the outer world. They effervesce later, again and again, but, however, make themselves more and more master of the thing. First, these self-workings out and, as we now already dare to say, "gestaltet" activities are directed toward the child's own body. With them the child busies himself and tries to accomplish as many as possible. He practices movements of the hands and of the arms; he lifts the head; he arches his body upwards till at length he stands and walks. All these are activities with which stimulation and guidance have little success so long as the child's own needs do not turn towards them. We name all these observed ways of behavior (already partly discussed in an earlier section from the viewpoint of positive or negative direction) in which not the success of the "approach" is intended but instead the success of activity is intended—we name these experimentative activities. That is, experimentally the child organizes his bodily movements, his stock of perception and sounds. He busies himself experimentally with countless manipulations of things and of each material which comes into his hands. Experimentally he becomes master of this material, makes it a tool for himself, and one day he constructs a new creation. It is a progress in the course of the development from the free activity of the uncoördinated purposeless movements of the first day to the organized purposeful building activity of the one year old child, a progress from a mere turning away or turning toward which effects the creative energy of the living.

THEREFORE WE DESIGNATE MOVEMENTS WHICH TERMINATE A STIMULUS BY A TURNING ASIDE, OR A TURNING TOWARD, BY FLIGHT OR DEFENSE, AS POSI-

The Spontaneous Reactions

TIVE OR NEGATIVE REACTIONS. WE DESIGNATE AS AC-
TIONS, HOWEVER, THOSE ACTIVITIES AND PERFORM-
ANCES WHICH DO NOT END IN THEMSELVES BUT GO
BEYOND THE "FORWARD TURNING" OUT TOWARD THE
OBJECT. With that we have, in general, an objective
criterion for the "moment of action" in the living
organism.

A survey of the development of the actions of a
child yields the following results:

1. THE IMPULSIVE MOVEMENTS. The spontaneous
activity of the newborn shows itself first in the impulsive movements which are distinguishable by their lack
of coördination and of regularity. They are never repeated in exactly the same way and order, but instead
are performed each time with variations and with very
many deviations. They are involuntary, not purpose-
fully directed, and do not receive attention or consideration. A criterion for their lack of coördination may
be the fact that it was often quite impossible, in spite
of the greatest effort on the part of the observer, to
follow a quite short sequence of movements in all their
complexity. To follow them merely by observations
with one's eyes and then by means of speech to describe them is well nigh impossible. Slow movement
cinema would here be necessary. We give you here several attempted protocols of the impulsive movements
of a thirteen-day-old boy:

B 70. The little hands are slightly balled; the little arms
which are likewise just a little bent travel about in the air; one
goes away from the chin, the other at the very same time hits
the chin; all fingers are in movement. The first three fingers of
the right hand are curled in, the other two at the same time
are stretched toward the back of the hand. The fingers of the

77

left hand flutter aimlessly without any sort of plan, each moves for itself, to and fro, in its own tempo.

Or: B 70 makes a fist, opens his right hand, flaps the index finger open and shut while the fifth and fourth fingers are stretched apart from each other and come together again. During this, the left hand is slightly curved, it travels restlessly and irregularly—slowly, then more quickly—a short way, a longer way—over the sheet.

A new situation: (It should be here noted that it was only after a whole system of signs for each observed portion of the body had been developed that we could observe and represent each possible successful movement.) The right hand passes over the mouth, the left, slightly curved, goes toward the left ear and the throat near by. The right hand travels for the first time over the length of the mouth on the underlip, then repeats over the nose, then over the chin. The fingers are stretched apart, then curved, the arms thrown now toward the front in the air (since the child lies on his back), the fingers move flutteringly—each for itself. Of the fingers of the right hand now two, four, and five are at the same time bent, and five and two stretched out again. With these movements of the hands, at the same time go, naturally, just as complicated movements of the head, the legs, and the toes.

We could at no time observe evidences of function pleasure accompanying these impulsive movements.

2. SINGLE MOVEMENTS ACCOMPANIED BY FUNCTION PLEASURE. At the end of the second month of life a whole series of movements of a new kind begin, which, like the impulsive movements, do not serve either the negative or the positive reactions. During longer or shorter periods, the child makes a whole series of single, unconnected movements. He turns his head, then lifts up a leg, purses his lips, moves a hand. These separate movements are different from the impulsive movements in that now a kind of certainty

takes the place of aimlessness and incoördination. These movements are often accompanied by mimicking expressional movements of function pleasure. They appear to be a transition from the entirely unintentional and aimless impulsive movements to the experimentative movements, which are characterized by intention and function pleasure.

3. THE EXPERIMENTATIVE MOVEMENTS. From the second month on, that child who by this time begins to give attention to his perceptions and vocalizations produces, in addition to those aimless movements and to those single movements accompanied by function pleasure which revealed an overflowing activity, a whole series of intentional movements which are coördinated and regular in progress. They were often repeated for a long time in exactly the same way and without any weakening. This regular repetition, the foresight and the care with which they are carried out (in contradiction to the impulsive and purposeless single movements), and the accompanying expressional movements of interest, all reveal the intention in which the child takes part. As they almost always appear to be accompanied by function pleasure, one can speak of these movements, according to the conception of Karl Bühler, as play. They lay claim to the intention of the child either because of the activity itself, or through the establishment of an aim as a midpoint of interest. In the first case we are concerned with a continuous experimentative activity; in the second case we have to do with an experimenting performance. The continuous experimenting activity is characterized by a repetition of a series of movements during a definite period; experimentative performance is characterized by new

79

movements which occur in the service of the attainment of the aim.

Experimenting activity occurs earlier than experimentative performance. The first experimenting activities confine themselves to the child's own body. Only at a somewhat later stage does there occur an activity in connection with objects in addition to the experimentings with his own body. The path of development is this: the child's experimentative movements are originally confined to his own body; then a quiet object is included in his play. Later he moves one or more objects in his play; and finally he brings about changes in the objects, and with them organizes new things.

4. CONTINUOUS EXPERIMENTATIVE ACTIVITIES WITH THE CHILD'S OWN BODY. We find that the two months old child performs continuous experimenting activities with his own body. At this time, we can observe the onset of a playing by means of the sense organs, the first playful practice with his own voice, the production of a succession of sounds, a repeated touching of the same object, a playful listening to his own vocalization, a playful looking back at objects. We call this behavior playful, because touching, looking, and listening are accompanied by function pleasure, and also because one and the same perception can be repeated, during a certain period, countless times. The continuous experimenting activities which are composed of a succession of regularly repeated movements, however, push the experimenting with senses far into the background.

There are a great number of possible variations of those movements which can occur as continuous experimenting movements. The distinguishable basic qualities on the other hand are limited in number. We find again in the experimenting movements those same kinds of movements which have already occurred as impulsive movements. We differentiate principally the following: stretching and curving of the limbs, the fingers, the whole body, the tongue and lips; raising and lowering of the limbs, the head, the shoulders, the back; turning the head, the arms, the legs, the hands; twisting of the fingers at the joints, and opening and closing of the eyes and of the mouth; a regular movement in a direction and back again, such as rocking, turning, etc. Besides those, there is the possibility for the single parts of the body to come together as in mere contact —pressing together, rubbing together, hitting one another, sticking into one another. We shall return later to these forms of movements which we find in the long succession of experimenting activities, and in playful practice of all movements which are connected with grasping. Since this experimenting is very soon directed toward objects and very seldom satisfied with the child's own body, we come soon to a manipulation of and with objects, a topic which requires separate treatment.

5. EXPERIMENTATIVE PERFORMANCES WITH THE CHILD'S OWN BODY. Whereas all those forms of single movements or groups of movements which have been discussed up to now classify themselves as aimless, the experimenting performances are directed toward a goal. From the negative reactions which were produced from the fifth month on, by the failure of an intended movement, we can see that the child very early appears to connect an intention with experimenting movements. We observed these for the first time in the newborn child in connection with posture

reactions. The newborn child knows only one negative reaction to posture. He answers every uncomfortable position with screaming and restless movements. We find the first active reaction to posture in the second month, when the head of a child who is lying on his stomach is lifted up, or if the child is lifted to a sitting position. The three months old child lifts his head and shoulders high out of the prone position. The five months old child when in prone position supports himself on his little hands only and lifts the lower arm up. The six months old child has the power to support himself on one hand in the prone position; he has achieved so much certainty that he can grasp with the other hand toward objects. Besides the reactions in the prone position there are still other posture reactions to be considered: sitting with and without support—this will not be mastered until the tenth month; standing with and without support, which the child begins to accomplish in the last months of the first year.

The child always reacts positively to a given posture much earlier than it is possible for him to seek this position himself. This means that the child can keep himself upright in a sitting position before he can sit up by himself. At the beginning, the positive reactions to posture claim all the strength of the child so completely that he cannot do anything beyond this.

Thus we find B 12:0;2 so busy with the lifting of his head out of the prone position that it is not possible for him to return the glance of his mother smilingly, as he usually does return it, if she bends over him and looks at him while he is lying on his back. At 0:3 he can already move his head in a lively fashion, attain the same posture, turn toward sound and sight stimuli, and laugh as soon as the glance of a grownup falls upon him.

B 35:0;7, completely busy with sitting in his bed, spies a

The Spontaneous Reactions

diaper on the night table. While his eyes are directed at it thoughtfully, he lifts one hand toward it and falls over.

For standing, we find a very enlightening example with G 45:0;9. She stands in her bed and holds herself firmly with one hand on the bedposts. With the other she reaches toward a ball which is being offered to her, and flops down in her bed.

The reaction to posture in a given position is, as we have already said, the preparation for a change in position. Here and there a "walzing,"[1] an extending and a stretching, a lifting up, are certain steps which precede a change in position. At four months we find the first attempts to shove forward and sideward in the prone position. These are seldom, as yet, successful. We now first observe a turning from the back to the side at the age of five months. At five months the child begins to raise himself out of the dorsal position. While lying on his back he lifts his head, he grasps toward objects, perhaps the railing of the bed, and attempts to pull himself up on it. At six months the child is able not only to turn from the back on to the stomach, but also to go back again from the prone position into the dorsal position. At the age of six months we find the successful forward movement, a kind of turning of the body from side to side forwards. At eight months the child, with assistance, raises himself to the sitting position and lies down again. At nine months the child sits without any help at all, and at the same time supports himself alone on the mattress. At eight months we find the first attempt to raise himself to a standing position, with assistance, and also at the same time the first successful creeping takes place. The attempt to creep, which was already begun by

[1] By "walzing" we mean a repeated roundabout movement.

four months old children, led to no success at the earlier time. At nine months many children walk with assistance. At one year many but not all children walk without assistance. Raising to a standing position, without help, was observed in 60 per cent of one year old children.

The following tables bring together our observations concerning reactions to posture, and reactions of the change of posture and position. [Tables VIII and IX.]

TABLE VIII

The Posture Reactions of the First Year

Age in months...................... 0 1 2 3 4 5 6 7 8 9 10 11 12

Holds head up......................	
Holds up head in prone position.......	
Holds up head and shoulders in prone position........................	
Rests on palms of hands in prone position	
Sits with assistance.................	
In prone position rests on only one hand	
Sits without assistance..............	
Stands with assistance..............	
Kneels............................	
Stands alone......................	

The child's experimenting performances with his own body can become continuous experimenting activities. They will often become so when the child is no longer completely occupied by them and when pleasure in the movement is experienced during the accomplishing of the movement. The first posture reactions are often accompanied by sounds of effort, by sighing and groaning. Alleviation of the tension, signs of comfort or pleasure occur only later, somewhat like the shouts of joy after the child sits upright. Since all the force of the child is given over to the reaction to posture, the movement of happy looking all about, often of rejoicing, becomes a movement of despair when the achieved goal is lost again. Only when the difficulties are no longer so great does the child experience pleasure in the movement of the posture reaction, and in change

TABLE IX

Reactions to Changes in Posture

	0 1 2 3 4 5 6 7 8 9 10 11 12
Age in months....................	
In prone position attempts to push forward with side movements.........	
Raises head and shoulders out of dorsal position........................	
Attempts to raise himself by aid of his hands..........................	
Turns from back to side.............	
Turns from prone to dorsal position...	
Turns from side to side.............	
Raises himself to sitting position without help.......................	
Successful crawling.................	
Raises himself to sitting position with help...........................	
Raises himself to standing position with help............................	
Walks with help....................	

of posture itself. And these movements become now incorporated as repeated movements, as groups of an experimenting activity. The examples here cited point this out.

B 320: 0; 7 contentedly rolls himself from one side to the other.

7.50 B 350: 0; 7 turns himself from his back to his stomach; grasps often on the railings of the bed while lying in prone position, lifting the head; tries to move himself completely
7.55 sidewards, but moves himself backwards; looks at himself, babbles; supporting himself on hands and knees he tries to go further; he is always in movement and sounds of effort accompany his activity.

8.05 Tries now to lay himself on his back; he is successful after several attempts; turns his head to and fro; lifts his arms
8.10 and lowers them again.

4.55 B 40:0;8 turns himself around to and fro in his bed with wide open eyes. He crows twice loudly, stands in his bed protected by his hands which clasp the rods, takes a step to and fro, rocks from one leg to the other, sits down, takes a rattle, shakes it holding it in the right hand, babbles and stops, screams with delight.

5.04 He is again quite quiet and busy with his play. Stands up again, seizes the bed railing with his hands, shakes here and there, sits down again; stands up again.

G 45:0;9 walks about in her bed with assistance, grasps toward the hand on which her rattle is hanging, sits down, stands up again, walks around again, seizes the bath towel which hangs near her bed.

These and the following observations show how, in a playing child, experimentative activities and performances—playing activities of the sense organs—playful practice of the already mentioned coördination of individual organs—are in many ways bound together and interrelated.

13.05 G 11:0;2 lifts her arm in the air and lowers it again. The fingers are at the same time stretched apart and
13.07 then curved. The arms are now stretched into the air and moved sidewards, and again bent. She lays her arms on the cover and puts her hands on her face. While the arms are now at rest, the head is moved. This all occurs with care, only the eyes wander about unsteadily.

13.10 The lips are moved, one laid over the other, then opened again. The tongue touches the lips and is again withdrawn. A door slams; she gives a soft cry, there is trembling of the eyes, of the entire body.

G 18:0;3 turns the head in a lively manner from one side to the other, lifts alternately arms and legs, stretches the arms and bends them again, follows a moving nurse with her eyes, yawns, rubs the index fingers together, sticks her right hand in her mouth, pulls it out again, and meanwhile gives forth soft cries of effort.

B 16:0;3 presses his hands on his mouth, lifts them again, then lifts the arms, curves his fingers, bends them, spreads them, stretches them.

B 12:0;2 sticks his fingers in his mouth, pulls them out again, looks then on all sides, goes on with his play.

G 22:0;4 moves her head to and fro, blinks her eyes, lifts her arm, turns her hands at the wrists, looks at them attentively.

7.18 G 21:0;4 follows her hands with an attentive glance,
7.26 lifts her arms, lets them fall on the covers again. As a nurse goes by she lifts her head and shoulders out of a dorsal position, lies there quietly looking till she becomes
7.40 restless, passes her hands over her face, turns her head
7.51 about, and cries. She quiets herself, sticks a finger in her mouth, pulls it out again, then lays one hand in the other alternately.

G 21 lifts the arms and lowers them again on the covers, follows them with her eyes, then lifts her head and lowers it, then touches the fingers of the right hand with the fingers of the left, stretches and bends the arms, lays one hand on the other.

G 24:0;4 presses one hand on the other, lets them go again. Lays her balled hands on her lips and lifts them off again.

B 29:0;5 lifts her hands to her eyes, observes them attentively. Stretches out her arms, bends them, follows them with her eyes.

15.02 G 22:0;5 shoves her hands into her wide open mouth, pulls them away again, lifts the right arm, follows it with her eyes, pulls the right hand back with the left and
15.15 pulls it out again. Lifts both hands to her face, moves again, moves first one finger, then the whole hand at the joints. Meanwhile, she kicks her legs in a lively manner.

We often find that a movement of the legs, an aimless kicking, accompanies a play or grasping of the hands. From six months on the legs also are included in the grasping play, and thereby in the experimenting.

G 30:0;6 stretches her arms contentedly in the air, grasps her shoes with her hands, turns herself then on her stomach and back again, grasps with both hands toward a leg.

G 31:0;6 turns her head again, pulls on the covers, lifts the hands high, lowers them again, grips the right foot with the left foot, lifts and lowers the two hands, holds the covers high. After she has lifted the covers several times she hits one foot with her hands, then beats with her fists on the mattress.

6. MANIPULATION OF AND WITH OBJECTS. The manipulation of and with objects, out of which later the conception of material form is developed, begins in that moment in which the touching, exploring hand of the two months old child glides over an object, attended by signs of attention. For yet a while longer the object remains unessential to the child. Occupation with his own body remains in the foreground, and the four months old child permits the rattle which he grasps with such care to fall, in order to continue experimenting with his own body, and he is satisfied with his own hands as play things. The most primitive sort of manipulation with which the child occupies himself is, we find, the manipulation of quiet objects—touching, holding, knocking, scratching, rubbing with the tongue, lips, hands, and little legs. With the exception of scratching, which appears to be specially difficult, we find all these activities before the fifth month. The development of manipulation of the moving objects goes hand in hand with the development of grasping. Through careful analysis of the observed cases we can

differentiate three principal, three fundamental, groups of activity practice. They are:

(a) The moving of objects which the child accidentally grasps or which have been put into his hand by the grownup—which need not necessarily be brought near the child. We can enumerate: shaking, lifting, lowering, moving to and fro.

(b) The bringing of objects near: grasping and seizing.

(c) The pushing away of objects: pushing away, kicking away, permitting to fall, throwing away.

We see at once that the activities of the first group are especially well adapted to be repeated as experimenting activities; those of the second and third groups occur as experimenting performances only if the child could already have accomplished these as experimenting activities.

The six months old child is no longer satisfied with playing with the object alone. He busies himself with one object, holding on to it and using it as though it were an elongation of his own hand, and he moves the object on a stationary object, knocks and rubs on it in the same way a four months old child had done with his hand alone. This onset—this doing something with an object—is the step preceding that of the use of tools. The seven months old child is able to play with two objects at the same time, either moving each separately, or knocking or rubbing one on the other. Pushing away and bringing close take place separately at this stage. When the child is seven months old, we find the beginning of a kind of activity with objects which is new in principle—an activity which through crushing together, pressing together, stretching, tearing, brings about a change in the form of the object. In these still destructive activities lie the first beginnings of form and shape. Definite "gestalten" reveal themselves in the attempt of the eight months old child to stick objects into each other, and in the first constructive trials of the eleven months old child to lay objects next to each other with care, and with pains to strive to stand them up. Up till this time the objects were carelessly thrown and permitted to lie where they fell. In the following somewhat short summary, we give you those observed types of activities with objects it will be recalled which occur in a definite order one after the other.

(a) Manipulation of quiet (unmoving) object with the child's own hand.

(b) Manipulation consisting in moving one object:
      1. moving
      2. bringing the object near
      3. moving the object away

(c) Manipulation of one quiet object with another moving one.

(d) Manipulation of two moving objects:
      1. to touch the one with the other
      2. to move both

(e) Change in form of the objects.

(f) Beginning of positive form—"Gestalt."

Besides those large steps here outlined, it is instructive to follow the way in which the lifting up and throwing away of an object gradually develops. We give here our observations:

0;4 An object is lifted and lowered.

0;6 An object is permitted to fall.

0;9 An object is lifted up and permitted to fall.

0;10 An object is lifted with one hand, grasped with the other hand and permitted to fall.

0;11 An object is lifted up and thrown forward.

7. ORGANIZED PLAY ACTIVITIES. From the seventh month, we can differentiate the play activities according to the particular parts of the body used in the play. The parts become active, one after another, according to a definite order. From the very beginning each separate part is regulated to the activity in somewhat the way the very first grasping occurs with both hands, and is not determined accidentally, nor through the kind of movement. Thus G 34:0;7 puts a little bandage from one hand into the other. B 36:0;7 sticks a bed cover into the mouth once with the right hand and then with the left. B 38:0;7 grasps his legs alternately with one and then with the other hand. The play of B 44:0;7 especially exemplifies this type of organized play activities. We emphasize also, however, that B 44 is exceptional in that his grasping play is especially well developed. In him we can confirm almost all possible variations of this kind of activity—shaking, hitting of an object first with one and then with the other hand, looking through an opening first with one and then with the other eye. Indeed, B 44 brought to a finish the business of changing a hand or foot alternately during an activity, by soon pushing toward a suspended object with his head, then with his foot. The organized activity of the child's own body appears to be a step preceding the organized play activities.

8. THINKING AS EVIDENCED IN THE USE OF TOOLS. We found the introduction to the use of tools, the beginning of making something with an object, demonstrated in the six months old child. With the nine months old child we could make several very valuable observations. An attempt was made to reach a fallen object with the hand—in vain. After several unsuccessful attempts to obtain it, a second play toy

was thrown at it. Considered alone, observations of this kind have no meaning. We can, however, study a whole series of other observations in this connection. The following observations will make this thought clear. We fastened a rattle to a long string on the bed of the children in accordance to an investigation which Karl Bühler has carried out with his own child and has written about. The ten months old children often fetched the fallen rattle with certainty by means of the string. They obviously established certain mechanical connections and brought about therewith a performance of "tool thinking" which probably is consummated entirely independent of speech. Similar performances have been observed in chimpanzees, and Karl Bühler has designated that period in the first year of life in which the child brings such performances, and practices to a successful conclusion, as the "chimpanzee age." In similar situations, performances such as the following were observed: at the age of ten months, seizing of the grownup by means of flowing apron bands; and at one year of age, the moving of an object, which lay too far to be able to be reached with his hand, by another object. If we take further notice of our observations of the nine months old child, then we can perceive as the first effort the attempt to come to a mechanical connection.

G 51:0; 10. The rattle falls to the ground. G 51 first looks at it with astonished expression, then she seizes the string in order to bring the rattle up, and pulls it toward herself with certainty.

G 63:0; 11 loses her handkerchief with which she is playing. She tries in vain to rescue it. Since in spite of all efforts she cannot get it, she seizes her pillow and throws it after the handkerchief.

The Spontaneous Reactions

With the entrance of this use of tools there begins an entirely new period for the child.

Very thorough and complete description of the childish play activities bring the following observations:

> G 22:0;4 pulls to and fro the rattle which her mother puts in her hand. Slowly and with regularity she raises and lowers the hand which holds the rattle. She shakes the rattle vigorously.
>
> 3.16 B 26:0;5 kicks the coverlet with both feet. He drags it about, then pulls it toward him. Then he lies quietly, observes his hands with which he alternately touches himself; then his left hand travels apparently purposelessly
>
> 3.24 over the cover; then with his right hand on the bed railing after he had turned himself on the side, he remains lying quietly while his hand clasps the railing.
>
> 13.00 B 26:0;5. A rattle is tied to a cord and fastened to the railing of his bed. He reaches toward the cord, first with his left hand, then also uses the right hand for this play, pulls at it with both hands, observes the band, which is twisted around his finger very closely. He shakes his rattle, views it attentively, allows it to fall sideways carelessly. As it is laid on his chest, he pulls again on the cord and plucks at it very carefully. By renewed pulling,
>
> 13.14 the rattle rolls over his face. He now pulls the cord with both hands, clutches the rattle accidentally and begins to shake it. Now he grasps the coverlet, which also serves as a sheet, and crushes it in his mouth. Lifts his head again, after turning himself into the prone position.
>
> G 32:0;6 plays with her cover. She pulls it over her face and pushes it off again. Then she lifts her covers with her hands and drops them; for a change she lifts them once in a while with her legs.
>
> G 30:0;6 with her hand grasps the celluloid ball which is suspended over her bed, catches the ring with the left hand, pulls backward and forward, catches it again with

the right hand and turns it over to the left. A rubber toy is shown to the child. She looks at it surprised, with large eyes and open mouth, takes it and tries to put it in her mouth, hesitates, turns on her stomach, lifts her head and shoulders upright, and tries to attract the attention of grandmother by her sounds.

G 31 : 0 ; 6 lifts her head from dorsal position. The rattle is handed to her. She grasps it with both hands simultaneously, holds on to the ring with her hand, reaches from a distance toward the ball, takes the rattle from one hand into the other. She brings the rattle, which she now holds by the ring along with the ball, near to her eyes, takes it away again. Again she holds the rattle in her hand quietly, in order to fetch the ball again and to try to pull it through the ring, which could not be done. She starts the other way around by trying to push the ring over the ball. She occupies herself only with the rattle, turns both rattle and ball in a lively fashion, throws the rattle from the bed, and looks bewildered toward her feet.

We will now give you in complete detail the play of B 45 : 0 ; 9 and a few other children throughout several hours. It should be here particularly noted, however, that B 45 : 0 ; 9 falls below the average in regard to posture reactions, and that therefore the grasping play, in his case, seems especially developed.

13.00 B 45 lies satiated in his crib, playing with his hands. Reaches for his cover and sheet, pulls it over his face and again removes it. With his little arms he hits his mouth quite severely, pushes his cover forward, reaches toward the sheet, drops it again. Moves his little hands over his face, observing them closely. Grasps the cover with both hands, loosens his grip with one hand and pulls it back with the other. He is now holding it with both hands, stretching it; crumples it again with one hand, trying with the other hand to get the end into his mouth.

The Spontaneous Reactions

He follows then with the playing of his fingers, stretches them out, closing them again into a fist. He pushes the sheet into his mouth, grasps with the one hand over the other and his mouth toward the sheet, seizes his rattle and shakes it, attempting to get it into his mouth. Sticks his hand through the ring of the rattle, grasps the ball with the same hand and moves with confidence. Sounds of comfort. The playing with the rattle is sometimes momentarily interrupted. Observer steps forward, observes the child and he smiles. On and off he breathes deeply, lifts his hand with the rattle quite high, eventually pulls the ring of the rattle from his arm, succeeding after several attempts. Now he takes the ring alternately from one 13.50 hand into the other. The ring is put into his mouth and he bites it. Both hands hold the rattle. He moves slightly and it falls from the child's grip. Now he reaches with both hands in the air, rubbing his eyes, kicking with his legs, one little hand in his mouth, the second closed on 13.52 his eye and again removed. Again the child follows with his eyes the play with his fingers—watching which one is being bent and stretched. He lies quietly, suckling, and he follows a passing nurse with his glance. The child notices an incoming nurse and with a surprised cry of amazement, joyful in its entire facial expression, accepts the rattle offered him. He grasps with one hand the ring, with the other the ball, and tries to separate one from the other. He pushes the ball and the ring into his mouth. As the cover is being removed he begins to reach with both hands toward his feet. He grasps the ball again, with which he beats on his face and smiles. He struggles joyfully with his little legs, trying with one hand, then with both, to put the rattle into his mouth, shaking it joyously. He continues playing with his little toes, stretching and bending. As soon as he succeeds in getting the ball near his mouth he bites at it. He now tries to put his hand and ring into his mouth simultaneously, pulls the rattle impetuously from one hand into the other, smiles

pleasantly and kicks off again the covers which were laid
14.05 on his legs. He allows the rattle to fall from his hand
on his face, picking it up again with the other hand. The
rattle is hidden under the cover. He can't find it, and
after some searching looks around quietly. Observer comes
near him, he smiles, expresses sounds of pleasure, betrays
signs of joyous surprise in his countenance, as he again
receives the rattle.

14.10 He moves his little arm through the ring, holds the ball
tight, and rattles. A child weeps. He begins to "lall."
One little hand lies quietly, the other he moves toward
the ball. He smiles to an approaching nurse, babbles some
sounds, interrupts his playing and follows her actions
14.15 with his eyes. Looks around, moving his head and his eyes.
Again he begins to search for the ball. It starts to rattle
suddenly, having been suspended quite high from the ring
near the shoulder. Pulls at the covers, but does not find
the ball. Rubs his eyes. The ball rattles, again he looks
for it. With one hand he gets hold of the cover and pulls
at it. He takes the ball, clutches it with his feet and holds
it, seizes it with his little hands, only to drop it again. He
begins playing with the cover, hands and feet participat-
14.25 ing. His feet are now resting on the cover. He mumbles
delightedly without any emotional excitement. Turns
sideways, seizes the sheet, accompanies his actions with
14.27 lalling sounds, grips the railings of his crib, pulling himself towards it, lifting thereby the upper part of his body
high, thus laying the weight on both his head and feet,
and in this way moves from this position. Sounds of comfort alternate with sounds of effort. Breathing satisfaction, he lies quiet. Now he begins a grasping play with
his feet. He seizes them alternately with his hands, mumbles delight, sucks his thumb and starts again with one
14.31 hand the grasping play with his feet. He utters sounds as
14.34 his lips press firmly one on the other. The playing with
feet being over, he seizes the sheet; the body turns sideways, the sheet being lifted high and dropped again. He

makes violent movements with his little hands, and satisfied sounds as the nurse enters the room. With an attentive eye he watches her actions, the inquisitive head lifted high and moved from the dorsal position.

14.34 He is overjoyed as the nurse comes near him. At her departure he lies quietly in his crib, shaking his head, a new play which gives him so much pleasure that he smiles.

14.49 Now he sucks his fingers, kicks again for a moment with his hands and feet, sucks further, occasionally lifting quite high the hand on which he is not sucking. He draws his hand from his mouth, turns sideways, turns back again, and again he begins to suck. One leg touches the bedstead.

14.55 He turns on his side, then he turns himself on to his stomach, lifts his head upright, places it down on the underclothes, stretches his legs and arms high, and ventures to move from his place because a black spot on the

15.10 wall attracts his attention. He attempts to move sideways, uttering therewith sounds of joy. He lies again on his back, his hands on his eyes, and begins to kick. He lifts his little legs high but not in as lively a fashion as heretofore. He discovers another sheet, places it on his

15.15 face and lalls while lying under it, turns sideways, pulls the sheet from his face, lies on his back, covers his face with his arms and lies motionless. The eyes are wide open. A new play now begins. The child puts his closed

15.20 fist on his lips and again removes it. From various heights he allows it to come down again. He is now through with

15.24 his play and views attentively the happenings in his room and the screaming of a little neighbor. He seizes the sheet, pushes it toward his mouth and away again, occupying, thereby, only one hand, and controls matters with his

15.36 eyes. He is lying again quietly, sucks his little hand, ready to fall asleep. He rubs his eyes and nose with his hands,

15.38 removes his finger from his mouth, puts it back again re-

15.40 peatedly. His eyes close; he sleeps, making some restless movements with his head and hands. He makes several movements in his sleep, breathes deeply and sleeps on.

15.44 The door being opened, he moves restlessly, stretches his little legs high, places his hands at his side and again on his face without opening his eyes. He utters a violent sound, puts a finger into his mouth, his eyes still closed.

15.49 He turns sideways and opens his eyes, lies on his back and looks around quietly. He sticks his finger into his mouth. The nurse comes near his bed, and he greets her with expressions of joy and with kicking. While being undressed, he utters sounds of pleasure and, as he again lies by himself, seizes the finger of his right hand with his left hand and pushes it into his mouth.

15.50 He observes closely the nurse arranging the room, barely moves; only his eyes wander as, through the glass wall, he notices some people passing. He rubs his eyes, lifts his hands, drops first one, then the other, on the sheet. He sticks his hands into his mouth, sucks them, removes them again, places them on the sheet and lifts them again. He lies

15.52

15.60 quiet, staring and sucking. He pulls his finger from his
16.30 mouth, seizes the railing of his crib with his hands, which calls his attention to the shadows of his hands. He fol-
16.37 lows these with his eyes. He seizes the rattle again, playing with it; he pulls it by the ring over his face, seizes the ring and the ball—each with one hand—and pushes
16.40 the ring from one hand into the other. He places himself on his side, holds the rattle by its ring in one hand and beats at it with the other. Now he lifts the rattle high and lets it drop again, changing it again from one hand
16.50 into the other, seizes the ring, holds the rattle high, and with one hand pushes the ball around the ring. Knocks
16.57 with rattle on the wall and enjoys the noise, laughing and crowing. The shadow on the wall has now attracted his attention. He follows it, lifting his little hands and dropping them again.

A new play: B 44 puts one finger into his mouth and withdraws it promptly. Alternately he puts his little fists on his face and removes them again. He turns

around, places himself on his stomach, supports himself
with the railings and begins lalling joyously. Then he
lies on his back fussing with the railings. B 44 gives out
three shrill cries, sticks his finger into his mouth and
begins to yell as the nurse comes near his crib. Tears run
down his face; he moves his hands restlessly around himself trying to put his finger into his mouth, continues to

17.07 yell, interrupts it momentarily, and begins again to yell.
He turns sideways, sucks his fingers for twenty seconds,
renews the yelling. He places himself on his back and
moves his hands restlessly; despairingly he tries to turn
his hands into a fist. The shrieking becomes more violent,
his little legs moving impulsively. He calms himself for
a few moments, moving his hand over his face and eyes,
and turns sideways. For a moment he discontinues to
yell, only to start again with renewed vigor. Then the

17.24 crying goes over into slight hiccoughs and he yells loudly.
Falls asleep, sucks his finger. He gives a slight shrieking,
and lies there with his eyes closed.

17.29 He is being prepared for his drinking, yells, quiets down
at once as he notices the bottle, starts to drink. He lies

17.35 quietly sucking one finger after the empty bottle has been

17.45 removed, pulls his hand from his mouth, stretches both
arms upright in the air for a moment, places them again

17.47 on the covers, seizes the covers with both hands. Suddenly he looses his grip with both hands. One foot lies on
the cover; the second, which is under the cover, lifts it,

17.53 picking it with his hands. Now his hands grasp his leg,
fussing with his toes; he pulls it toward his face. The
child laughs, overjoyed with pleasure, mumbles, seizes his
little leg at the knee, pushes his legs under cover, lifts
his cover with his legs high, laughs at it, his hands not

18.03 participating in this performance. The little legs are tired
of play. An end of the sheet, which is fastened in the
middle as a girdle, is seized and dropped again. Both legs
are now being pulled from under cover; the cover is
being pushed into a corner. He seizes it with his legs

and pulls it forward. He places the soles of his feet one against the other, rubbing them, the toes of one foot touching the other, the little arms making simultaneously

18.10 some slow movements, being stretched and bent. Then he lies again quiet, outstretched sideways in his sheet. The

18.16 little legs are now being lifted and dropped. He stretches his hands toward them. The child now turns sideways, places himself again on his back, puts his little hands into his mouth, withdraws them again, smiles at me, as I look at him. He grasps with his hands, over his head, toward the railing. He is making an attempt to pull himself up. He places his little hands one on top of the other, pressing

18.19 them closely together, places them on his mouth, then on his ears, uttering sounds of joy, which turn into a slight

18.21 lalling. Now he begins to pull his little shoulders around; the sounds which accompany his activity are quite lively. He succeeds in grasping his shirt, he pulls at it, quite

18.25 pleased, lalls joyfully, pulling at his shirt. The cover is again brought forward with his little legs, assisted by his little hands. He is babbling all the while. The right hand he sticks into his mouth, the left on his forehead. He sucks, babbles, stares. He kicks furiously; he moves his little hands accompanied by the clicking of his tongue. He seizes the rattle again; with one hand he grasps the ball, with the other the ring, changing it alternately from one hand into the other. He licks the ball with his tongue. Now he shakes his rattle first to the right then to the left,

18.33 lifts it high and with a swift grasp places it in his mouth. He holds the ring, beating his own face with the ball. He seizes the ring with the other hand and throws the

18.40 ball down on the sheet. He touches the ball with his lips,

18.42 shaking it violently by the ring. The rattle travels from

18.44 one hand to the other. He rattles with bodily strength, lifting the ring high, and moving the ball to and fro. He now places the ring, alternately, on his face, and his eyes,

18.46 looking through it. He drops the ball. The child lies quietly on his side, moving his little hands slightly, pick-

The Spontaneous Reactions

ing at his jacket and little shirt, following his movements
18.50 with attentive eyes. He puts one little hand into his
mouth, with the other he scratches the cover. He opens
and closes it again. He places his little arms over his face
and babbles pleasantly. He sucks his finger, ventures to
lie on his stomach in order to observe a black object more
closely, tries to grasp it with his hands after turning side-
18.55 ways again. He turns around again, seizes the railing
tightly with one hand, lies on his left side, bending his
19.01 head backward, kicks to and fro with his legs, grasps the
railing and reaches for the cover. He grips with his hands
through the railings of his crib, changes his position; thus
occupied, he observed the railings closely. After putting
19.09 himself on his back, he seizes the rattle and shakes it violently. He turns again sideways, pushing himself toward
19.11 the grating, beating it impetuously with his hands. He
grasps quickly toward a railing, letting it loose promptly.
19.16 Now he lies quietly on his back, moves his head, first
right, then left. Seizes occasionally the railings, on which
he keeps his eyes, and beats with his right hand at the
19.21 wall, putting it then into his mouth. Sucks quietly on his
finger, keeping his eye on the cover. He turns again to
his right, grabs the railing with both hands, and pulls
himself toward it in a highly convulsive manner. With
19.28 his little hands he beats on his mouth, turns sideways,
seizes the railing with both hands and pulls himself toward it. The legs kick the cover off, assisting, thereby,
the little hands. Puts a finger into his mouth, places himself quietly on his back and looks around. Starts a grasping play with his leg, grasps it with his hands, drops it
again, babbling at the same time joyously. Ceases to
babble, the grasping play continues with his feet. Inquisi-
19.32 tively he pursues the movements of the toes. One little
foot tries to seize the rattle. The child rolls himself fur-
19.50 ther sideways, tries to sit up, lies down again and looks
around. He makes several movements with his little arms
and legs, and falls asleep.

G 45 : 0 ; 9, in contrast to B 44, can change her position more easily. Her play has therefore a quite different aspect.

G 45 receives a ball, takes it alternately with her right hand and with her left hand. It is still necessary that she
9.00 support herself with one hand against the railing so as not to fall over. She puts the ball in her crib and reaches
9.05 toward a cloth which hangs suspended near the crib. She reaches for the end of the night table, stretches herself, standing again in her little crib. Finally she sits down. She seizes with both hands the ball which is still lying
9.07 in her crib, holds it with one hand, beating it with the other. Rolls the ball through her little legs here and there, takes it again from one hand into the other. Leaves the ball lying, gets up again, crawls, sits down again, tries to remove the gold-red stripes from the ball. She stands up again and walks around in her crib, utters several forcible sounds. Reaching again for her cloth she
9.15 babbles in a lively manner, picks at her ears, stands in her crib with one finger in her mouth, seizes the ball which is offered to her, sits down, utters several pleasant sounds, observes the ball, lifts it high, throws it down,
9.45 places herself on her stomach, crawls around in her crib, stands up again.

G 39 : 0 ; 11 has now a plaything in her hand and lalls
12.07 loudly. She is quiet, sucks on a band, and allows sounding air to stream from her lips. She has the plaything in her hand, shakes it here and there, tries to sit up and, as
12.12 she succeeds, jumps in her little bed to and fro. She stands up in her crib staring. A wimble falls down. She
12.15 bends in an effort to pick it up, crying, not being able to reach it. The sheet is being picked up. G 39 is very quiet. She stands observingly. Sometimes she mumbles to herself. She is being taken into the arms by her mother, smiles and is very happy, kicking and lalling. Placed on

12.30 the floor she tries to walk by herself, holds on to the table, carefully loosens one hand, tries to do the same with the other hand, but quickly recaptures it, having
12.31 lost her balance. She is now led around the room by her mother. Taken into the arms and brought near the windows, she knocks at the window, babbles continually,
12.31 laughing and kicking. Set on the floor, she crawls around, seizes a plaything and plays. She enjoys herself thor-
12.47 oughly. She lifts the doll, puts it down again and looks
12.55 around. Now she crawls on all fours searching for playthings. Not finding any, she utters sounds of displeasure.
13.00 She finds the doll, calms herself, beats the floor with the doll, places it from one hand into the other, thus keeping
15.00 herself occupied. The mother calls her; she listens and answers, "da." She continues playing, lifts the doll, puts it away quite surely and definitely, only to grasp it again
15.22 just as surely. She is quiet and very happy, babbles considerably, sits upright in her crib, pulling down a sheet; sits down, gets up again, stands and looks about. Utters several sounds of displeasure, lies down, straightens herself up again, sucks on the railings. She babbles and moves to and fro in her crib. Tries to reach a picture which hangs on the wall and moves on. Now she touches the colored stripes on the ball and continues babbling. She is being set on the floor and plays with a trumpet. She puts it into her mouth and then tries to put the trumpet into the ball net. Being thus occupied she is quite fresh and lively, and being observed or smiled at, she babbles in return. She shakes the trumpet up and down in her hand. Now she shrieks into the opening of the trumpet, lays the trumpet aside, and tries to crawl around on her knees.

CHAPTER VII

Reactions to the Taking of Nourishment

SUCKLING is indeed one of the few instinctive acts which the human child performs almost completely from the beginning on. In the first weeks of life the child may be made to produce suckling movements by the mere contact of an object with his lips or the neighborhood of his mouth. Suckling can be called forth even in a sleeping child if the lips are accidentally touched—let us say by the child's own moving hand. For all that, we find that a child who is completely asleep will accept food only in the first months of life. However, until the child is seven months of age, he will quite often fall asleep while taking food, and in this case often drinks his bottle empty, although he is asleep. The newborn child who is busy with the taking of food has fists slightly curved, arms bent, eyes usually closed, and he is entirely busy with swallowing and sucking.

The performance connected with the taking in of food becomes more and more complicated during the first year of life. The child of one month, when brought to the lap of his mother, turns his head toward the breast.

For this behavior Bechterew makes the gradual effect of the memory of the vertical position of the child on the mother's lap responsible, whereas Preyer and Stern take into consideration the memory of the smell and sight perceptions. This same situation causes

the child of two months to search the breast with restless movements of the head and with pursing of the
lips. The same behavior can also occur when the bottle
out of which the child was drinking slips away. At five
months the child clasps the bottle with his hands while
drinking, and cries as soon as he spies the bottle. In
the same way the child of this age, when being fed
with a spoon, opens his mouth as soon as the spoon
comes near. Until then the mouth would open only
when the nipple actually touched the lips. Indeed, the
child of six months sticks the bottle in his mouth himself. At eight months the child brings the thing which
he is eating to his mouth, and, if at age of four months
he had already begun to bite and at seven months to
chew, he bites of it. At nine months the child waits
quietly when preparations for feeding are commenced.
Until then, the child exhibited great displeasure if he
could see the food which was slow in being offered to
him.

Examples of the described ways of taking nourishment:

B 8:0; 1, who sleeps, opens his eyes, starts to move, and to
twist his head. Sleeps again. While sleeping he drinks his bottle,
the top of which has been put to his lips, half empty. He doesn't
wake, and makes no other movements aside from the suckling.
Again he falls asleep without further suckling, although there
is more milk in the bottle.

B 5:0; 1 is laid on the lap of his mother. He immediately
turns his head toward the breast; drinks as soon as the nipple
is put into his mouth, with strong pulls. The arms are bent, the
fists lightly curved.

B 5:0; 1. Taken by the mother in her lap he immediately
begins to make sucking movements. The nipple is pushed into
his mouth, he sucks on it strongly. He falls asleep, leaves off

sucking. The mother moves his head to and fro several times; he opens his eyes again, and begins to suck. He closes his eyes gradually and, sucking, he falls asleep. Stops sucking.

B 10:0;1 sleeps. The bottle is pushed into his mouth. He starts sucking it with closed eyes. He drinks all his milk. The bottle is taken from him and the sucking movements cease. He opens his eyes and lies quietly with his eyes open. He falls asleep again.

B 12:0;2 with restless movements of the head and stretching of his lips seeks toward the nipple. The hands are lightly clutched on his own chest. B 12, on being given tea, opens his mouth when the spoon touches his lips, clicks his tongue, licks his lips with the tongue.

B 26:0;5 as he sees the bottle starts again to get uneasy, to scream, to make restless movements of the arms, of the head, of the legs. The bottle is given to him and he drinks with strong effort. The hands clutch the bottle. Licking of the tongue, denoting comfort, fills little pauses which arise between the individual tugs at the bottle. He drinks it all. He kicks the railing as he moves sideward; the bottle, which he lets go, rolls toward the side.

G 28:0;5. At the sight of the bottle she starts to struggle, to cry. She quiets as the bottle is pressed into her mouth. She falls asleep while taking her meal, stops sucking though there is still some left in the bottle.

G 30:0;6. Puts the nipple of the bottle, which she misplaced in order to take a look at her approaching mother, again into her mouth.

G 45:0;9 sits crying in her bed, facing the soup which is placed on the table. She holds tight to the railing of the bed, raises herself, moves in her bed to and fro grumbling. She gets her soup to eat. Sits up quietly in her bed as the nurse gets near her with the plate. She allows herself to be fed. Pushes the spoon aside and spits out the offered soup. As soon as the nurse absents herself she adjusts herself in her bed and moves about to and fro. When the nurse leaves the room, in order to refill the plate with vegetables, she starts to cry out loud. She quiets herself immediately as soon as the nurse enters the room again with the replenished plate. She sucks quietly on her finger, and watches the nurse who feeds a second child. But when the nurse is through feeding the other child and does not turn toward her but turns instead toward a third child, she starts to cry as usual until the nurse turns toward her. With a happy babbling she greets the nurse as she comes near her.

B 44:0;9. At the sight of the bottle he starts to cry. As he is made ready for his drink and the napkin adjusted, he is at once quiet.

The newborn child is so busy with the taking of its nourishment that he pays no attention to any other attraction. Smacking of the tongue and sounds of joy accompany his taking of food. At the age of two months, the child keeps his eyes open a little longer while taking nourishment. At four months we find sounds of comfort uttered in the small interrupting pauses during suckling. At five months the child turns his head during his meal to the grownup. From this time on, slight sound and sight stimuli interrupt the child while feeding, and he will even smile at the person who gives him his food. These observations permit of the conclusion that the child is no longer so exclusively occupied by his greediness for food.

The satisfied child stops suckling even if the suckling itself produces further stimuli. We have examples in the recorded protocols to confirm this statement. But the one month old child already experiences a new negative reaction to the taking of food, which in itself does not interfere with the positive reaction to suckling. The child is no longer satisfied with mere suckling movements, but draws his head back from the source of nourishment and pushes out the breast or the nipple with his tongue.

G 11:0;2 is handed the bottle. Without opening her eyes she begins to suck. She pushes aside the bottle in which there is a little left. Uneasily she moves her head, her hands, her eyes.

G 19:0;3 is through drinking; she turns her head sideways.

B 16:0;3 is no longer hungry. He spits out the nipple, then a little milk, and quietly he lies there observing.

12.52 G 21:0;4 wakes as the bottle is pushed into her mouth. Drinks, pauses occasionally in order to smile at nurse who holds her bottle.

13.11 Pushes from her mouth the bottle, in which there is still a little left. She puts her arm around the bottle in her effort to push it away. Then she stretches, lifts her arms and stretches them out.

B 20:0;4, a child who drinks tea, pushes the bottle aside with his hands and cries.

That the self-retreat from the source of stimulation, the turning aside of the head when satisfied, occur earlier than the turning aside of the defense movements can be observed in still other fields. Charlotte Bühler was the first to call attention to the greater difficulty of defense movement as compared to flight movement.

The satisfied child often stretches his body and his head at the same time as he turns his head aside (0;1). He gives an impression of satisfaction as shown by a quiet, comfortable condition of waking. The aspect of the hungry child is quite different. He displays great unrest, and is in continual movement. The child who is ill-humored from one cause or another makes noticeably strong suckling movements without any sucking object touching the lips, and he is further characterized by a trembling movement of all the soft parts of the face—of the mouth, the chin and the lips. The crying

Reactions to the Taking of Nourishment

is very loud, but it is always interrupted by suckling movements. Hungry children attempt to change their

TABLE X

Ways of Behavior in Taking Nourishment

Age in months	0 1 2 3 4 5 6 7 8 9 10 11 12
Sucking when lips are touched by objects	
Gulping	
Licking	
Occasional sounds	
Turning the head toward the breast	
Searching for breast with movements of the head and pursed lips	
Biting on different objects	
Unrest at sight of the bottle	
Opening of mouth as soon as the spoon approaches	
Bottle clutched with the hands	
Bottle nipple pushed into mouth	
Chewing	
Holding and biting of things to eat	
Quiet at sight of preparations for feeding	

TABLE XI

Ways of Behavior in Condition of Satisfaction

Age in months	0 1 2 3 4 5 6 7 8 9 10 11 12
Discontinuance of suckling movements	
Vomiting	
Spitting	
Drawing back of the head	
Pushing out the nipple of the bottle	
Stretching of the body	
Irregular movements in the direction of the bottle	
Pushing aside of the bottle	

postures much less often than children who are out of sorts for any other reason.

We can often observe negative reactions when the

child eliminates the feces—movements, screaming, and expressional movements, and also sounds of effort which accompany the activity of the stomach pressure. The screaming in the aforementioned situation is to be characterized as a cry of pain. The contact of "wet" after urinating as well as the touch of the soiled napkin causes the child to give forth negative reactions. Even this varies with the individual.

CHAPTER VIII

Sleep and the State of Dozing

SLEEP is the outstanding condition in the progress of the day of the newborn child. The condition of being quietly awake is, indeed, in these first weeks only a sort of semi-consciousness. Despite the great amount of sleep, we could see, in exact observations, that the sleeping periods are very short. The longest uninterrupted, unbroken periods of sleep which we could observe are shown in Table XII.

TABLE XII

Age	0 ; 0	0 ; 1	0 ; 2	0 ; 3	0 ; 4	0 ; 5	0 ; 6	0 ; 7	0 ; 8	0 ; 9	0;10	0;11	0;12
Longest period of uninterrupted sleep (in min.)....	220	221	292	373	361	312	354	550	520	570	524	600	569

We can see that the uninterrupted sleep duration which is from nine to ten hours occurs first in the child's seventh month. Preyer, Aschaffenburg, and Cerny have already recorded the remarkably short continuous sleeping periods of the suckling. The sleep of small children, asserts Aschaffenburg, reaches its greatest depth very quickly, mostly in the first hour. The young suckling child wakes regularly after two to three hours, only to fall asleep again.[1] Whereas we find that

[1] Denissova and Figurin have made precisely the same assertions, having observed two newborn children from birth on for nine days, by

in older children a lesser sleep depth turns to a deeper sleep depth, the suckling awakens each time. It is surprising how long it takes children to get accustomed to a long uninterrupted night of sleep. In spite of the removal of every distraction they still hold fast to their short sleeping periods.

As we have already described, we established precautionary measures during our observations, so as not to disturb the child by a light while he was asleep. On the other hand, however, in keeping with the spirit of observation, normal sleep disturbances were not excluded. Every increase of the length of the longest uninterrupted sleep duration is accompanied by a limitation of the number of sleeping periods, as can be seen by a comparison of both illustrations.

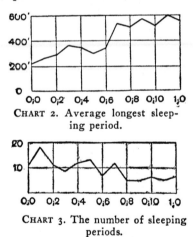

CHART 2. Average longest sleeping period.

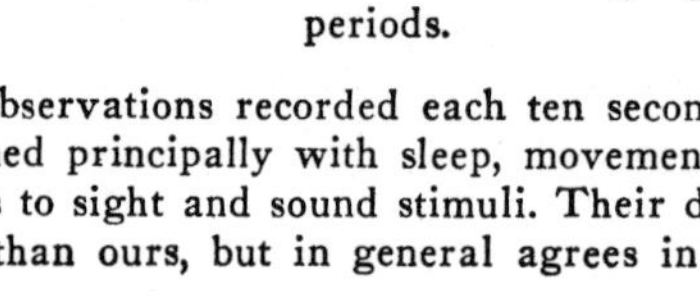

CHART 3. The number of sleeping periods.

day and night, observations recorded each ten seconds. Their conclusions are concerned principally with sleep, movement in feeding, skin reflexes, reactions to sight and sound stimuli. Their description, as yet, is less complete than ours, but in general agrees in the essential observations.

Sleep and the State of Dozing

The average number of the sleeping periods in the first quarter of the year amounts to twelve, in the second to eleven, in the third to seven, and in the last quarter of the first year of life, to six. Quite surprising are the very short sleeping periods of only a few minutes, which we find in all children. They are to be recognized by their quiet regular breathing and complete relaxation of all muscles. These short periods, although lasting only two or three minutes, actually cause a sleeping condition. This is very evident from the fact that the children who gave a tired and inactive impression before the sleeping period appear fresh and lively afterwards.

By dividing the sleep into twenty-four hours, we establish the following time dates from the information obtained from a few of our protocols:

B 3:0;0 (+ 6)		G 21:0;4		B 56:1;0	
7.00- 7.22	22	7.00- 7.45	45	13.45-15.11	86
7.31- 8.30	59	10.16-10.25	19	18.00-19.20	80
8.50- 9.20	30	11.32-12.05	33	20.02- 5.10	538
9.31-10.45	14	12.07-12.11	4	5.55- 6.00	5
12.15-12.25	10	12.45-12.48	3	11.20-12.15	55
12.29-12.45	16	14.11-15.30	79		
12.52-14.49	57	15.40-15.54	14	Number of sleeping	
15.05-15.12	7	16.05-16.38	33	periods—5.	
15.15-15.25	10	16.40-17.03	23		
15.28-15.30	2	18.35-18.57	22	Value of daily sleep	
15.33-15.40	7	19.10-19.19	9	—764 minutes.	
15.45-16.08	23	21.10- 3.30	380		
16.10-17.49	39	3.59- 4.45	46		
18.51-19.00	9	4.58- 5.00	2		
19.06-19.25	19				
19.35-21.14	99				

B 3:0;0 (+6)　　　　G 21:0;4　　　　B 56:1;0

21.19-21.33	14
21.56- 1.20	204
1.35- 2.00	25
2.15- 3.45	90
3.52- 7.00	188

Number of sleeping
periods—14.

Value of daily sleep
—712 minutes.

Number of sleeping
periods—21.

Value * of daily
sleep—944 min-
utes.

　* By "day value" we mean, as we have already explained in Chapter I, the sum of the time duration of all the separate periods devoted
to any one group of behaviors that are alike in character taken during
the twenty-four-hour observation period.

7.00　B 1:0;0 (+ 1). Sleeps. Trembles as the cover is momentarily removed, makes several restless movements.

8.15　Sleeps on. Cries out softly, then cries louder, opens his
eyes only a slit wide, then sleeps again. Takes the bottle
as it is pushed into his mouth.

8.41　Makes several suckling movements.

8.47　He sleeps again. The bottle is again pushed into his
mouth. This time he makes three or four more suckling
movements.

8.55　Fast asleep. Moves in his sleep without outside reason.
Opens his mouth while asleep.

10.20　Gulps quickly several times in succession.

10.51　Again opens his mouth wide.

10.55　Aimlessly he moves his arms up and down his face.

11.15　Falls asleep quietly again. Impulsive movements of the
arms interrupt the immovability of the child. He is then
taken from his crib, dressed for the doctor's visit, and put
on the swaddling table. He cries loudly.

16.00　B 4:0;0 (+ 6). Sleeps.

Sleep and the State of Dozing

17.40 Moves arms. Makes sounds of discomfort, moves his lips in sucking fashion without opening his eyes for a moment. Quietly he continues sleeping.

17.55 Begins to cry. Moves his arms and legs restlessly. Light is put on.

18.12 Wakes and lies there with his eyes half open. The slits between the lids become smaller and smaller. Sleeps.

7.10 B 50 sleeps. Opens his eyes, twists his head to and fro, cries very gently. Lies down again with closed eyes.

7.15 Moves his head restlessly, begins to cry lightly, sleeps on.

7.19 Rubs his face with his fist, lifts his covers with his hands restlessly.

7.22 Continues to sleep. Opens his eyes, yawns, turns his head. Sleeps.

7.30 Makes a slight sound; the hands move restlessly; sleeps on.

7.35 Breathes deeply, turns his head, sleeps on.

8.10 Sleeping, he is carried to the swaddling table. Opens his eyes, lies quietly looking on.

12.00 B 12:0; 2 sleeps with fists pressed on his chin; he makes a few restless movements in his sleep.

13.06 The hands are laid on the napkin with which the mother covers his head. He utters a few sounds.

14.00 The arms move restlessly. The fists move, rubbing his eyes and nose; remain again lying pressed against the chin. Restless head movements.

14.05 Sleeps, makes a few light sounds, raises his eyes, stretches his mouth open. Rubs his eyes with fists, makes groaning sounds, stretches his arms.

14.06 Screams.

The picture of a sleeping child becomes an ever more quiet one. Already at the age of three months we have periods of more than an hour in which nothing occurs which would disturb a quiet sleep.

18.42 G 19:0;3 falls asleep; sleeps deeply and quietly.

19.01 Opens her eyes and stares quietly around. Begins to scream.

19.07 Moves her head restlessly to and fro, kicks with arms and legs.

19.23 Tries vainly to turn from her position. In midst of the lively sounds of displeasure, she quiets herself and lies down tired.

19.30 She falls asleep, breathes regularly, quietly.

20.10 The bottle is handed to her while asleep.

20.22 She begins to suck, through the contact of the nipple on her lips.

20.22 The empty bottle is removed.

20.29 Still makes slight sucking movements in her sleep. Normal quiet sleep.

24.16 Breathes deeply. Wakes and starts to kick and to scream. She is wrapped around, during which she does not cease her sounds of displeasure.

24.19 Dried and covered, she ceases the sounds of displeasure. She lies quietly.

24.21 Stares with open eyes toward the cover.

24.41 Sleeps deeply and quietly.

24.45 Opens her eyes again, and again stares at the cover.

 1.20 Starts to scream, and to move her head and limbs restlessly.

 2.00 Lies inactive with eyes wide open. The eyes close gradually; she sleeps.

 3.54 Is awakened to take her meal. She is at first wrapped up, opens her eyes, glances around, drinks with open eyes, after the nipple is pushed into her mouth, until the bottle is empty.

 4.02 As the empty bottle is removed her eyes close.

 7.00 Sleeps quietly and soundly.

19.00 B 53:0;10. Sleeps.

19.22 He is adjusted in his crib. He stands up crying and marches around the crib. The nurse lays him down again. He rebels, screaming and kicking. Finally he remains lying quietly. He is huddled up, pressing his face into the pillow. Sucks his fingers.

19.55 Falls asleep.

21.24 Screams, lifts his body, has his eyes open, puts head and shoulders, which he lifted high, down again. Sleeps on.

23.14 Sleeping, he is wrapped up.

4.11 Stands up in his crib suddenly, wide awake. Sticks his thumb into his mouth, walks around his crib. He must support himself with his right hand, which he does not suck.

4.16 He touches the rods of his crib and babbles at the same time.

4.18 Lies down again, slowly closing his eyes.

4.25 Deep regular breathing betrays that he is fast asleep.

6.20 Wakes up, stands up in his crib and screams.

B 53 shows us not only the progress toward long periods of perfectly quiet sleep, but his behavior is typical of children who have just learned to stand. As soon as he awakes we see him standing in his crib. Indeed, in the evening the nurse has trouble to bring him to a state of rest. The ability to stand means so much at first, as we can also see in other children, that they always want to stand and they struggle against sitting down. It happened once that a child fell asleep while standing, was awakened by the lying down and after displaying many signs of displeasure, straightened himself up again.

We see that the sleeping periods become always longer, and the sleep always quieter. When one disregards the outer sleep disturbances and recognizes only the ones in the child himself, one realizes, as Chart 4 shows, that those which at first played an important part have in the fourth month of his life already become meaningless. Just how far the occasional impulsive movements and sounds accompany the sleep or actually disturb it, one cannot state positively. The numbers used in Chart 4 refer to every ten sleeping hours of a certain stated age. The newborn child is invariably receptive to outer disturbances of sleep. He becomes frightened at heavy noises, sudden touch, and changes of temperature such as occur when covers are lifted. The actual awakening that is often followed by sounds of displeasure comes, all in all, first at the age

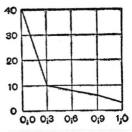

CHART 4. Frequency of the inner sleep disturbances without waking within 10 sleeping hours.

of one month. To measure the effect of outside sleep disturbances does not lie within the bounds of our research.

The preferred sleeping position of the child in the first year of his life remains as that of the embryo. The fists lie slightly bent near the head. The knees are somewhat stretched, the soles of the feet, at least the big toes, lie one on the other. If perchance a finger, a hand, or a wrist, fall in the child's mouth, it is sucked. The child takes the same position in a quiet waking state. Only when the child is four months old does one notice a different sleeping situation. From then on we find the child lying on his side, or in the prone posi-

118

tion, stretching his arms and exhibiting innumerable other variations, even if the original position for sleep and the state of wakening still retain the preference. We find very often that the newborn child takes nourishment while asleep. Beginning with the eighth month this is no longer to be observed. Facts which depend on probable dreams we could not ascertain nor establish.

To the ways of behavior during sleep belong also the reactions of falling asleep and awakening. The newborn child twitches in that moment when he falls asleep. This was for us a sign which made it possible to recognize the already mentioned sleeping periods of a few minutes as sleeping periods. The two months old child often turns his head sideward just when he falls asleep, the four and five months old child makes a sideward movement with his whole body. Awakening, the newborn child throws his head backward, stretches his arms and his body. The one month old child moves his arms and fists over his face with uncertain movements. The five months old child begins to rub his eyes.

The signs of fatigue are yawning, sleepy expressions of the face, lusterless and half-closed eyes. The lifting of the heavy sinking eyelids we find first in a two months old child, while the other signs of fatigue remain the same from the first to the last day of the first year of its life. The child who has made progress in the ever increasing mastery of his movement exhibits one characteristic sign of oncoming fatigue—that is, the slowing up of his movements, a behavior which is similar to the impulsive movements.

In B 4:0;0 (+6) we noticed that yawning occurred when the child was fatigued. B 12 shows the typical picture of the awakened child, throwing his head backward, moving his fists restlessly over his face and eyes, stretching out the arms. Out of these quite aimless movements which already occur in a newborn child, later comes the rubbing of the eyes and nose with the fist. For the child who is falling asleep there are two more characteristic reactions: a small spasm often moves through its entire childish body the moment it falls asleep; and from two months on the head is often turned strenuously aside. Later, there occurs a turning of its entire body.

13.18 G 11:0;2. As eyes close, she sleeps.

13.20 A child coughs, G 11 opens her eyes, closes them again ever so quickly and sleeps.

13.21 Opens her eyes with several sounds of displeasure, turns her head. One arm is drawn toward her breast and again pushed off. The legs lift up the covers several times. Her head moves restlessly to and fro. Her lips are pressed together and again separated.

13.25 The eyes close. The head turns impetuously toward the right side (she lies on the left). The hands are stretched out, lying quietly clenched near the head, the mouth slightly open. The eyelids are slightly raised, soon sinking again. The child lifts her eyelids again somewhat.

13.22 The head is turned in her sleep, and laid backward. She opens her eyes, yawns, twists her head, stretches out her

13.36 hands, yawns, sleeps on. She turns the head; eyes are

14.10 again open. Moves her hands; sleeps. Restless head move-

14.14 ments because of clattering of crockery near by. Opens

14.20 her eyes, closes them again instantly. Moves and stretches. Several sounds accompany her action. She opens her

14.23 eyes, swallows and sucks several times. Utters sounds, looks around, begins to cry aloud.

Very similar to sleep is a quiet—that is, motionless —state of being awake, which is accompanied by

TABLE XIII

Sleep and Its Transitional Periods of the First Year of Life (Brief Summary)

Age	Longest Sleep Period	Number of Sleep Periods	Disturbances	Behaviors			
				During Sleep	While Falling Asleep	Awaking	In State of Fatigue
0;0	220	11	40	Lies in fetal position; impulsive sounds and movements; suckling movements; reactions to surrounding stimuli. Takes nourishment while asleep.	Convulsive movements.	Throws head back; stretches head and body.	Facial expression lax; lack of luster of the eyes, yawning, slow closing of the eyes.
0;0 0;3	312	12	10	"	At 0;2 throws head back violently.	Fists and arms travel about over the face with uncertainty.	Raising and lowering of the eyelids.
0;4 0;6	342	11	8	Lies in other positions besides the fetal position.	Turns body sidewards.	Stretches body and hands. At 0;5 definite rubbing of the eyes.	Movements become slower and more uncertain.
0;7 0;9	548	7	5	Few impulsive sounds and movements. No longer takes nourishment while sleeping.	"	"	"
0;10 1;0	564	6	2	Impulsive sounds and movements entirely disappear.	"	"	"

121

neither positive nor negative movements of expression, and which we designate as dozing, since it does not seem to be characterized by those ways of behavior which otherwise give meaning to state of being awake. Dozing is characterized by the sleepy facial expression and lack of luster of the eyes. It often occurs between two periods of a state of waking, in somewhat the same way as the before-mentioned few minute sleeping periods. Children appear to be quite as rested after the finish of this dozing period, as they are after a few minutes of sleep. But it also introduces a change of conditions from one kind of period to a different kind. For instance, it can occur as a transition between the periods of screaming and the periods of function pleasure with accompanying single movements, or it can lead from the waking condition into sleep. The quiet dozing plays a very important rôle in the first half of the first year of life, but later, as we shall see, it recedes into the background and becomes less important in meaning. To close, we present the description of several observed cases of dozing.

12.04 B 10:0;0 (+ 1). After being unwrapped, B 10 is placed back again in his bed. He blinks his eyes, permits them to remain quietly open, and lies there with open eyes. The muscles of the face are relaxed and slack, the eyes are dull. Only very seldom, in intervals of several minutes, does he make a slight turning of the head or a light movement of the hands.

12.15 One hand accidentally touches his lips. B 10 begins to suck on his finger (fourth right). The eyes are moved;

12.16 they do not squint but look about in coördinated fashion. B 10 stops sucking. The finger remains on his lips, the

12.30 eyes are wide open. Not a movement is made. He pulls his finger out of his mouth, opens and closes the eyes several times with backward, irregular movements, whereby the eyelids of both eyes move independently of each 12.35 other. B 10 lies there again quietly looking. The eyelids 12.38 gradually close; he sleeps. Trembles as he sleeps.

7.00 B 20:0;4 lies in his crib. Rubs his eyes with his hands; 7.02 lies quietly there, awake. No movements. The eyes close. One arm, bent, is laid near the head, the other lies on the cover. B 20 sleeps. While sleeping makes an up and down movement of the hand.

10.42 B 52:0;10 lies quite still with wide open eyes.

10.50 After he has been lying so quietly he closes his eyes and softly dozes.

10.58 Falls fast asleep.

CHAPTER IX

Summary of the Behavior Forms of the First Year of Life

BEFORE giving a summary of the behavior of children, there is still something to be said about "single reactions." By "single reactions" we mean those reflexes and perceptions which do not occur included within an activity or action, but which themselves constitute a complete act. If you call activities and actions a "mentally directed event," then the single reactions and impulsive movements are, in contrast, not mentally directed. Although the child does not yet lead (as does the grownup) a life determined chiefly by tasks and problems, and his day is not yet a sequence of almost entirely predetermined events, still in the second half year of nis life, consciously determined actions prevail over the undetermined ones. Only in the first half year do the single reactions, which from the viewpoint of the grownup and the already active playing of the one year old child seem disturbances and incidents, exceed regular sequences and unities of behavior.

The single reflex movements and perceptions which actually appear as independent events are generally momentary reactions to sudden and disturbing stimuli.

We have tried to arrange and to count all the ways of behavior, so far described, according to the point of view of the scheme established in Chapter I. Primarily, we have counted the numbers of periods during the day for ways of behavior, similar in any way.

Behavior Forms of the First Year of Life

For this accounting we have used four age-levels: the newborn, the three months old, the six months old, and the one year old child. The results are shown in the following table:

TABLE XIV

The Relative Proportions of the Periods of Various Behavior
Units (in per cent)

Age	0 ; 0	0 ; 3	0 ; 6	1 ; 0
State of Rest (Sleep and Dozing)	19	20	14	12
Single Reactions	66	33	23	19
Impulsive Movements	2	10	12	—
Total	68	43	35	19
Functional Activities	—	12	19	29
Performances	13	25	32	40
Total	13	37	51	69
Grand Total	100	100	100	100

This table may, to a certain extent, be considered more instructive concerning the facts of the first year of life than most information as yet obtained on this subject. Let us look at it separately.

TABLE XV

The Proportional Relation of the Sleeping and Dozing Periods
to the Periods of Behavior (in per cent)

Age	0 ; 0	0 ; 3	0 ; 6	1 ; 0
Sleep and Dozing	19	20	14	12
Waking Behavior Periods	81	80	86	88
Total	100	100	100	100

At first, sleep and the similar state of dozing show the already known decrease in quantity, and although the newborn sleeps 80 per cent and the one year old 50 per cent of the day (see Table XII, Chapter VIII), nevertheless the newborn goes through eighty-one different periods of behavior during the nineteen periods of sleep. In this quantitative relationship there occurs no important change. A look at Table XIV, however, shows us that, though the total number of periods does not vary, their nature and distribution varies completely with different ages.

TABLE XVI

The Proportional Relationship of Observed Periods of Directed and Undirected Events (in per cent)

Age	0;0	0;3	0;6	1;0
Single Reactions	82	41	28	22
Series of Behavior—Impulsive Movements	2	13	15	—
Total	84	54	43	22
Continuous Activities	—	15	22	33
Performances	16	31	35	45
Total	16	46	57	78
Grand Total	100	100	100	100

While the newborn shows 75 per cent single reactions, increased slightly by impulsive movements, the one year old shows more than 75 per cent of continuous activities and actions. The change from a majority of single reactions and impulsive movements to a majority of continuous activities and actions clearly occurs between the third and sixth months; and according to all results so far obtained probably around the fifth. While the three months old child still shows 54 per cent single reactions plus impulsive movements, the six months old child shows already 58 per cent of continuous activities and actions. Significant changes in the quantitative relationship of ways of behavior also take place in the first quarter and in the second half of the first year. The increase of directed behavior (periods of activity and action) from 16 to 46 in the first quarter of the year is as significant as the decrease of non-directed behavior (single reactions and impulsive movements) from 43 to 22 in the second half.

Finally, we can formulate the course of development of the child by saying that the non-directed behavior of the newborn is related to that of the one-year-old in the ratio of 4 to 1; the mentally directed behavior in the ratio of 1 to 5. Already in the second half year of human life the mentally directed actions exceed those not directed.

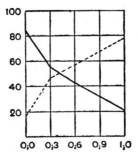

CHART 5. The percentual relation between directed and undirected acts.

——— undirected
- - - - - directed

The principle according to which the single, observed ways of behavior were included in this system can be found in the following grouping on which our accounts are based. In the first group, containing the states of sleep and the state of rest, we counted a period of sleep together with the previous falling asleep and the subsequent awakening; we counted the period of dozing and one period of quiet waking as a transitional state between two different periods. As single reactions we treated as disturbances of sleep such effects of sensory stimuli as the blinking, opening and shutting of eyes, tossing about of the head, shrinking and fright. At a higher stage, we include also some reactions to perceptions, such as a quick looking at the stimulus, a short listening, grasping reflexes, etc. As sequences of behavior we found periods of impulsive movements and sounds, habitual crying, periods of continuous experimental activity, periods of lalling, and of receptive and contemplative waking. The first units of behavior which we could already observe with certainty in the newborn were the taking in of food, followed by a reaction of satiation, and periods of active ill-humor. In addition to these there are the reactions of flight and defense, reactions to position, experimenting performances with objects, grasping performances, and expressional movements of astonishment, fear, expectation, and desire.

Individual behavior is discussed in the Inventory (pages 170-185), where we give still more detailed information.

CHAPTER X

A Quantitative Analysis of the Observed Behaviors

THE qualitative analysis of the observed ways of behavior which we have made so far, describes the different steps in development, sequence of their appearance, the changes which we find during the first year, and the time at which these changes occur. We were also able to determine exactly how much time in a day was taken up by each different way of behavior and calculate a "day value." By "day value" we mean the sum of all the time devoted to the combined periods of the similar behavior within a day's observation. There are two examples of 24-hour-long observation presented in Gesell's *Mental Growth of the Pre-School Child.* Here, too, the attempt is made to count up the periods of similar behavior. But his groups have been established in an uncontrolled method and they lack a relation to one another. We shall presently describe our attempt at solution, which was not confined to a separation according to external factors. As we have already mentioned, Denissova and Figurin watched the two newborns uninterruptedly for nine days.

First of all we will have to separate the behavior during the sleeping state from that of the waking state. The numerical results of this separation can be seen in the following two tables:

TABLE XVII

The Average Duration of the Sleeping and Waking States
Within 24 Hours (in Minutes)

Age	0;0	0;1	0;2	0;3	0;4	0;5	0;6	0;7	0;8	0;9	0;10	0;11	1;0
Sleep	1152	930	864	802	883	701	766	726	798	767	652	744	738
State of Waking	288	510	576	638	557	739	674	714	642	673	788	696	702
Total	1440	1440	1440	1440	1440	1440	1440	1440	1440	1440	1440	1440	1440

TABLE XVIII

The Duration of the Waking and Sleeping States Within 24
Hours (in per cent)

Age	0;0	0;1–0;3	0;4–0;6	0;7–0;9	0;10–1;0
Sleep in per cent	80	60	55	53	49
State of Waking in per cent	20	40	45	47	51
Total	100	100	100	100	100

If the day value for sleep seems unexpectedly small in these tables, it is because in our observations we could detract the periods which interrupted the child's sleep, periods which are frequently unobserved and are therefore included in the duration of sleep.

We consider the decrease of the duration of sleep and the increase of the waking state to be the basic condition for any growing development, for it means a broadening of the time in which strength can be developed. The greatest decline of the sleeping curve is noticeable during the first quarter of the year. Twenty-one per cent of the daily value for sleep of the newborn is lost in that time. From the third month to the end of the first year, the curve for sleep loses only 7 per cent more of its daily value. The fifth month is

decisive in that the sleeping and the waking states are
evenly divided over the day.

The waking state can be either quiet or occupied by
some sort of movement. The various forms of quiet

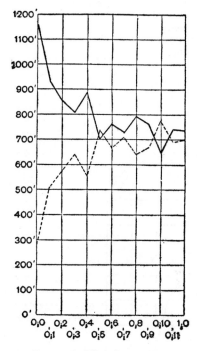

CHART 6. The day value for
sleep and waking in minutes.
——— sleep
- - - - - waking

waking we have already characterized. The day value
for the dozing state, which in the newborn takes up
100 per cent of the quiet waking state, fills only 53
per cent of that of the one-year-old. We can observe

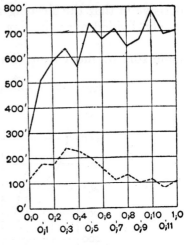

CHART 7. The relation between active and quiet waking periods.
———— active waking
- - - - - quiet waking

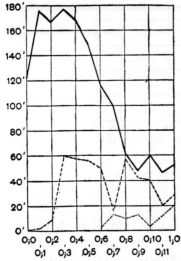

CHART 8. The distribution of the different forms of quiet waking in relation to the day value of quiet waking.
———— dozing
- - - - - positive quiet waking
...... negative quiet waking

the decisive change, the sudden decrease of the dozing state, in the eighth month. This is shown in the following table:

TABLE XIX

The Day Value for the Different Forms of Quiet Waking
(in Minutes)

Age	Dozing	Condition of Comfort	Receptive and Contemplative Waking State	Quiet Displeasure	Total in Minutes
0 ; 0	123	—	—	—	123
0 ; 1	176	2	—	—	178
0 ; 2	167	2	7	—	176
0 ; 3	177	3	57	—	237
0 ; 4	168	1	56	—	225
0 ; 5	147	2	54	—	201
0 ; 6	117	4	45	—	166
0 ; 7	100	1	15	3	119
0 ; 8	61	2	55	13	131
0 ; 9	47	2	39	10	98
0 ; 10	66	3	38	13	114
0 ; 11	46	1	20	8	75
1 ; 0	53	2	26	20	101

We notice that from the second to the third month that part of the day value for quiet waking which is taken by the receptive waking state now increases. With the appearance of contemplative waking, the part of the receptive and contemplative waking state

133

increases percentually once again, only to lose in significance once more during the last quarter of the first year. This can be explained by the fact that the child

TABLE XX

The Percentage Proportion of the Several Forms of Quiet
Waking in Relation to the Daily Value for Quiet Waking

Age	Dozing	Condition of Comfort	Receptive and Con-templative Condition of Waking	Quiet Displeasure	Total
0 ; 0	100	—	—	—	100
0 ; 1	99	1	—	—	100
0 ; 2	95	1	4	—	100
0 ; 3	79	7	24	—	100
0 ; 4	72.5	2.5	25	—	100
0 ; 5	72	1	27	—	100
0 ; 6	70	3	27	—	100
0 ; 7	84	1	12.5	2.5	100
0 ; 8	46.5	1.5	42	10	100
0 ; 9	48.5	2	39.5	10	100
0 ; 10	52.5	2.5	34	11	100
0 ; 11	50.2	1.5	27	10.5	100
1 ; 0	53	2	26	20	100

now reacts with active interest to all sense perceptions
and no longer meets them in a quietly receptive state.
The decrease of the dozing state can be traced through
the entire first year. While the quiet waking state of

A Quantitative Analysis of Observed Behaviors

the newborn was filled up entirely by dozing, from the eighth month on only half of that state is thus occupied. The state of quiet displeasure, which increases, fills about one-quarter of the quiet waking of the one-

TABLE XXI

The Average Day Values for the Different Groups of Behavior (in Minutes)

Age	Sleep and Dozing	Negative Reactions	Positive Reactions	Spontaneous Reactions	Total
0 ; 0	1,275	104	47	14	1,440
0 ; 1	1,106	237	73	24	1,440
0 ; 2	1,031	187	89	133	1,440
0 ; 3	979	179	121	161	1,440
0 ; 4	1,051	171	124	94	1,440
0 ; 5	848	159	129	304	1,440
0 ; 6	883	122	126	306	1,440
0 ; 7	826	146	93	375	1,440
0 ; 8	859	99	155	337	1,440
0 ; 9	814	83	113	430	1,440
0 ; 10	712	101	135	482	1,440
0 ; 11	790	57	92	510	1,440
1 ; 0	791	77	112	460	1,440

year-old. It increases because the state of restless displeasure decreases. From among the forms of quiet waking we join together the state of dozing and sleep, putting them into a common group. Both decline considerably during the first year of life. In the same degree in which sleep and unoccupied waking decrease, the waking state, which is filled with impressions and actions, increases. The latter is usually a state of movement, seldom one of rest. In connection with our quali-

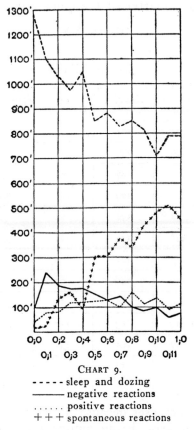

CHART 9.

- - - - - sleep and dozing
————— negative reactions
. . . . . . positive reactions
+ + + spontaneous reactions

tative analysis we tried to calculate the day value for the three different groups of reactions—for the negative, positive, and spontaneous reaction. The day value thus estimated is shown in Table XXI.

Comparing these results we find decrease of day value for sleep and dozing, during the first year of life. Decisive changes take place between the fifth and tenth months. After reaching a maximum in the first month there is a decrease of negative reactions, and an increase of positive reactions from the first day of life. The greatest day value increase, however, is found in the part given to spontaneous reactions. In these, the fifth and ninth months reveal an especially great development. What time-proportion each of the four groups of behavior occupies in the day of the newborn, the half-year-old, and the one-year-old, can be seen in the following table. This table shows the

TABLE XXII

The Part (in per cent) Taken by the Various Reactions in the Course of the Day

Age	Sleep and Dozing	Negative Reactions	Positive Reactions	Spontaneous Reactions	Total Per cent
0 ; 0	88.7	7	3.3	1	100
0 ; 3	76.8	12	8.2	11	100
0 ; 6	56.1	8.4	8.5	27	100
0 ; 9	57.5	7.3	7.7	28	100
1 ; 0	55	6.4	7.6	31	100

enormous growth of positive and spontaneous reactions. The spontaneous reactions of the newborn take up 1 per cent of the day, and of the one-year-old, 31 per cent of the day. This last-mentioned fact is evidence of the growing activity of the developing child.

Some additional facts concerning the increase in daily values can be obtained from Table XXIII.

TABLE XXIII

The Day Values of the Separate Groups of Behavior (in Minutes)

Age	Sleep	Dozing (Transitional States from Excitement to Quietude)	Defense, Flight, Screaming	Quiet Displeasure	Taking Food	Movements of Approach and Grasping Toward Sensory Stimuli	Social Approach	Receptive (Contemplative) Waking	State of Comfort (Joy)	Random Aimless Movements. Impulsive Sounds	Experimentation Lalling	Total
0;0	1,152	123	104	—	46	1	—	—	—	14	—	1,440
0;1	930	176	237	—	70	1	—	—	2	24	—	1,440
0;2	864	167	187	—	77	2	1	7	2	122	9	1,440
0;3	802	177	179	—	53	2	6	57	3	117	46	1,440
0;4	883	168	171	—	53	6	8	56	1	64	30	1,440
0;5	701	147	159	—	51	13	9	54	2	108	196	1,440
0;6	766	117	122	—	53	13	11	45	4	104	205	1,440
0;7	726	100	143	3	48	14	14	15	2	73	302	1,440
0;8	798	61	66	13	65	10	18	55	7	21	316	1,440
0;9	767	47	73	10	35	15	14	39	10	—	430	1,440
0;10	652	60	88	13	61	12	17	38	7	—	482	1,440
0;11	744	46	49	8	43	14	8	20	7	—	510	1,440
1;0	738	53	57	20	48	13	14	26	11	—	460	1,440

A Quantitative Analysis of Observed Behaviors

As negative reactions we distinguish two groups: negative movement, and negative expressional movements alone. We see that in the first half year negative movements of expression never occur by themselves. We have figures to prove the statement, already made, that the elementary and most important reac-

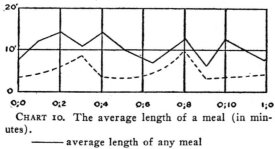

CHART 10. The average length of a meal (in minutes).

——— average length of any meal
- - - - - average length of breakfast

tions of the child reveal a great activity, and that passive ill-humor is only a later form of negative reaction, growing always less significant. The positive reactions divide into the following groups: reactions to feeding and sensory stimuli. These reactions take form in grasping, social approach, receptive waking and positive expressional movements. The daily value for feeding cannot show any development, since it differs according to the individual and depends on the sort of food and its preparation. The variation of the child's dependence upon the immediate need of nourishment is shown by Chart 10, in which we compared the length of the breakfast, often already impatiently awaited by the child after the long night's rest, with the duration of any other meal. The average time needed for consuming the breakfast is sometimes only

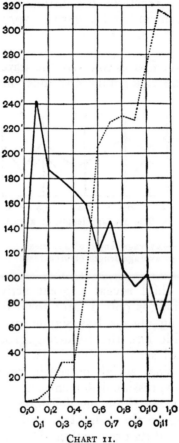

CHART II.
——— negative expressional
movements
...... positive expressional
movements

one-fifth the time needed for another meal of equal quality and quantity.

As long as it is only a movement toward a sensory

stimulus, the reaction of approach and grasping plays a subordinated rôle. The decisive change is made during the fourth and fifth months corresponding with the development of grasping. That social approaches increase with time is explained sufficiently by a previous statement concerning the number of social reactions at various states. The decrease of the day value for receptive and contemplative waking during the last quarter of the first year, which is the result of the awakening active interest, has been mentioned as well. The day value for positive movements of expression grows during the second half year of life, when some active expressions of joy can be observed in addition to a quiet waking state of comfort. We have observed that this quiet state of comfort is a condition first accompanied by positive expressional movements and only much later accompanied by the active outbreaks of joy, while negative reactions, on the other hand, show the quiet expression of ill-humor much later than active utterances. The appearance of these active outbreaks of joy also produce the sudden increase in positive movements of expressions between the fourth and sixth months. That the behavior expressing joy increases during the first year is shown clearly by Table XXIV.

All the periods in which positive or negative movements of expression were observed, irrespective of whether they were the dominating factor or just different ways of behavior (experimenting, single movements, reception of food), are here grouped together according to time and contrasted with each other. We can state concerning them that positive expressions appear much later than negative ones, and that, although

at first they are far less than the negative, they finally
exceed them considerably during the first year.

TABLE XXIV

The Duration of Observed Positive and Negative Expressional
Movements (in Minutes)

Age	Positive Expressional Movements	Accessory Pos. Exp. Movements	Total	Negative Expressional Movements	Accessory Neg. Exp. Movements	Total
0 ; 0	—	—	—	104	—	104
0 ; 1	1	—	1	232	—	232
0 ; 2	2	10	12	187	—	187
0 ; 3	3	29	32	179	—	179
0 ; 4	1	32	33	171	—	171
0 ; 5	2	92	94	159	—	159
0 ; 6	4	201	205	122	—	122
0 ; 7	2	223	225	146	—	146
0 ; 8	7	222	229	99	8	107
0 ; 9	10	218	229	83	10	93
0 ; 10	7	264	271	101	2	103
0 ; 11	11	306	317	57	10	67
1 ; 0	11	300	311	77	21	98

The spontaneous reactions include two groups: aimless movement and impulsive sounds in one group,
experimenting and lalling in the other. The aimless
movements increase in frequency with the decrease of
the negative movements which have reached their

maximum daily value in the first month. They decrease in that moment when the observed experimenting movements begin to broaden. Experimenting, which fills 11 per cent of the waking of a two-month-old, occupies 63 per cent of the waking time of a one-year-old.

TABLE XXV

The Percentual Relation of the Daily Values for Positive and Negative Movements of Expression

Age	Negative Expressional Movements	Positive Expressional Movements	Total in per cent
0 ; 0	100	—	100
0 ; 3	87	13	100
0 ; 6	37	63	100
0 ; 9	29	71	100
1 ; 0	25	75	100

TABLE XXVI

The Average Maximum Duration for Some Groups of Behavior (in Minutes)

Age	Dozing	Neg. React. (Defense Flight Screaming)	Random Movement	Experimentative Movements
0 ; 0	19	16	11	—
0 ; 3	40	48	33	18
0 ; 6	44	38	22	40
0 ; 9	48	26	12	40
1 ; 0	14	20	—	143

The day values of the groups just discussed are composed of many different periods. (Concerning the number of these periods compare Chapter IX.) Regarding the question of a child's perseverance, which is generally considered to be very little, it is valuable to observe how long a child occupies itself voluntarily with one and the same thing. The maximum duration of some groups are given in Table XXVI.

The maximum periods of dozing, of negative reactions (movements and expressional movements), and of aimless movements grow shorter and shorter; the periods of experimenting and lalling grow always longer. The perseverance of the one-year-old who spends an uninterrupted two hours and twenty-three minutes in experimenting is especially remarkable. We can also find a great progress in perseverance during the last quarter of the first year. If we measure the various groups of behavior according to time, we would find: decrease of sleep, increase of waking, lessening of quiet waking, especially of dozing; decrease of negative, increase of positive and spontaneous reactions; growth of positive expressions—a general increase in positive and active behavior.

How the duration of the varicus groups of behavior is distributed during the day can be seen in the following typical diagrams which we call day cycles. The circle corresponds to the 1,440 minutes of the day; the values of the various groups are entered as sectors. In these diagrams we can study the forward steps in development as easily as in graphs and tables.

CHARTS 12-18. TYPICAL DAY CYCLES
EXPLANATION OF LEGEND FOR CHARTS 12 AND 13:

| Sleep | Dozing | Negative Reaction | Taking Food and Approaching Movements | Spontaneous Reaction |

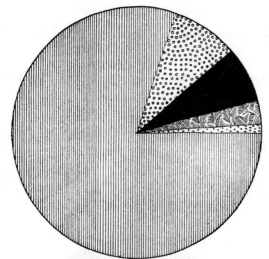

CHART 12. Typical day cycle, age 0; 0.

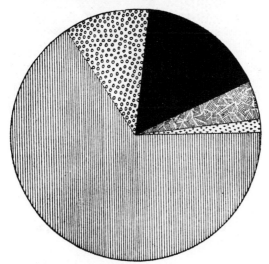

CHART 13. Typical day cycle, age 0; 1.

LEGEND FOR CHARTS 14-30:

Sleep

Dozing

Negative
Reaction

Taking Food

Approaching
Movements

Positive
Quiet Waking

Impulsive
Movements

Experimen-
tation

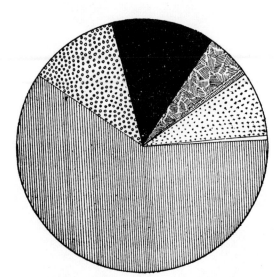

CHART 14. Typical day cycle, age 0; 2.

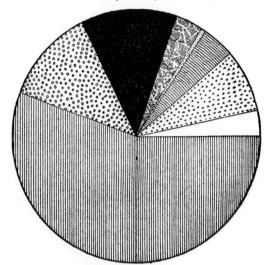

CHART 15. Typical day cycle, age 0; 3.

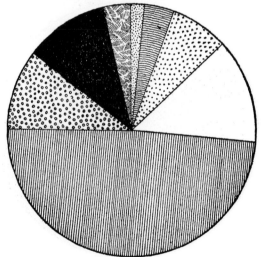

CHART 16. Typical day cycle, age 0; 5.

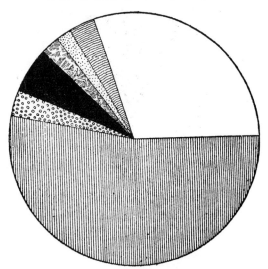

CHART 17. Typical day cycle, age 0; 9.

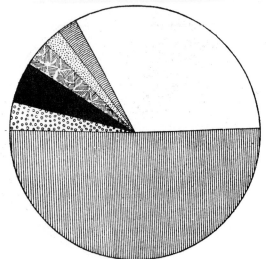

CHART 18. Typical day cycle, age 1; 0.

CHAPTER XI

Individual Day Cycles and Developmental Progress

THE following examples show the individual daily events of separate children as we could observe it in a newborn, a two months old, and a seven months old child. Those single reactions which seemed merely intermediary were not considered here. The letters written next to the time of day are to be read as follows:

S—Sleep

NS—Taking of food during sleep

N—Taking of food

R—Quiet waking, D in parenthesis—dozing, P—receptive and contemplative waking and state of comfort.

U—Negative reaction

B—Aimless movements

Ex—Approaching movement and experimentation.

B 10;0 (+ 1)

7.00- 8.15 S	13.11-13.17 NS	17.45-17.49 R
8.15- 8.23 U	13.17-15.25 S	17.49-17.52 U
8.23- 8.41 Ex	15.25-15.36 B	17.52-18.45 S
8.41- 8.55 NS	15.36-15.45 S	18.45-18.47 NS
8.55-12.00 S	15.45-15.55 NS	18.47-19.58 S
12.00-12.04 U	15.55-15.56 S	19.58-21.05 U
12.04-12.30 R	17.15-17.24 B	21.05-21.09 B
12.30-12.40 B	17.24-17.36 R	21.09-21.15 R
12.40-13.11 S	17.36-17.45 B	21.15-22.30 S

22.30-22.40 NS	23.03- 3.06 S	6.14- 6.24 NS
22.40-23.02 S	3.06- 3.17 NS	6.24- 7.00 S
23.02-23.03 U	3.17- 6.14 S	

Day Totals

S	....	1,203'
NS	....	63'
R	....	48'
U	....	83'
B	....	43'
Total	....	1,440' = 24 hours

G 14:0;2

9.10- 9.28 S	13.50-14.15 S	18.00-18.17 R (D)
9.28- 9.35 R (D)	14.15-14.17 R (D)	18.17-19.00 S
9.35-10.20 Ex	14.17-14.31 S	19.00-19.15 N
10.00-10.48 B	14.31-14.45 U	19.15-19.21 R (D)
10.48-10.54 R (D)	14.45-14.47 R (D)	19.21-21.48 S
10.54-10.59 U	14.47-14.54 U	21.48-21.55 N
10.59-11.04 S	14.54-15.07 R (D)	21.55- 4.19 S
11.04-11.05 U	15.07-15.35 U	4.19- 4.28 N
11.05-11.08 R (D)	15.35-15.58 S	4.28- 4.42 R (D)
11.08-11.35 S	15.58-16.03 N	4.42- 6.45 S
11.35-11.45 B	16.03-16.10 R (D)	6.45- 6.48 B
11.45-11.51 U	16.10-16.20 S	6.48- 7.07 R (D)
11.51-11.58 R (P)	16.20-16.24 U	7.07- 7.40 B
11.58-12.15 S	16.24-16.34 S	7.40- 7.45 B
12.15-12.27 R	16.34-16.45 U	7.45- 7.50 R (D)
12.27-12.30 U	16.45-16.54 B	7.50- 7.55 B
12.30-12.45 N	16.54-17.25 R (D)	7.55- 8.20 S
12.45-13.36 B	17.25-17.35 U	8.20- 9.02 R (D)
13.36-13.50 R (D)	17.35-18.00 S	9.02- 9.10 S

Day Totals

S	884'
N	61'
R	207'
(P 7' D 200')	
U	99'
B	164'
Ex	25'
Total	1,440' = 24 hours

B 35:0;7

7.00- 7.12 Ex	10.55-11.00 R (5P)	16.15-16.37 B
7.12- 7.15 U	11.00-11.05 Ex	16.37-16.42 U
7.15- 7.25 Ex	11.05-11.10 U	16.42-16.45 B
7.25- 7.30 L	11.10-11.25 Ex	16.45-16.46 U
7.30- 7.55 Ex	11.25-11.26 U	16.46-17.00 Ex
7.55- 8.05 U	11.26-11.27 R	17.00-17.09 N
8.05- 8.35 Ex	11.27-11.40 Ex	17.09-17.10 U
8.35- 8.42 R (7P)	11.40-12.22 S	17.10-17.25 Ex
8.42- 8.54 U	12.22-12.40 U	17.25-17.30 R (5P)
8.54- 9.01 S	12.40-12.58 Ex	17.30-18.05 Ex
9.01- 9.06 U	12.50-13.15 N	18.05-18.10 R
9.06- 9.16 N	13.15-14.20 Ex	18.10-18.48 S
9.16- 9.25 Ex	14.20-14.22 R (2P)	18.48-19.20 Ex
9.25- 9.34 U	14.22-14.30 Ex	19.20-19.25 U
9.34-10.02 S	14.30-14.32 U	19.25-19.29 N
10.02-10.06 U	14.32-14.45 R	19.29-19.35 R
10.06-10.23 S	14.45-15.02 S	19.35-19.55 B
10.23-10.25 U	15.02-15.21 S	19.55-20.25 S
10.25-10.35 B	15.21-15.22 U	20.25-20.35 R (10P)
10.35-10.37 U	15.22-15.30 R	20.35-20.40 S
10.37-10.51 Ex	15.30-15.38 U	20.40-20.42 U
10.51-10.52 U	15.38-16.00 Ex	20.42-20.44 S
10.52-10.55 Ex	16.00-16.15 U	20.44-20.50 U

20.50-20.55 R	3.50- 4.00 U	6.01- 6.10 L
20.55- 3.05 S	4.00- 5.27 S	6.10- 6.30 U
3.05- 3.30 R	5.27- 5.34 N	6.30- 6.42 R (12P)
3.30- 3.50 L	5.34- 6.01 B	6.42- 7.00 B

Day Totals

S .... 662'
N .... 47'
R .... 104'
(P 46' D 58')
U .... 148'
B .... 100'
Ex ⎞
L ⎭ .... 279'
Total .... 1,440' = 24 hours

The time won by the decrease of sleep is distributed, if we compare the daily sum of the newborn with that of the two-month-old, almost equally over the quiet and the occupied state of waking. The expressions of ill-humor experience merely a very slight increase.

If, however, we compare the daily sum of the two-month-old with that of the seven-month-old, we see that all time-values, including those of sleep and feeding, lose in favor of one single factor—namely, that of experimental movements which are accompanied by function pleasure. These have increased more than ten times during the five months.

Similar individual day cycles are represented by charts 19-30. They show that the newborn has fewer periods of directed actions during the day and that these periods increase in the course of the first year.

We consider it especially advantageous that we were able to observe the same child at different age-periods

Day Cycles and Developmental Progress

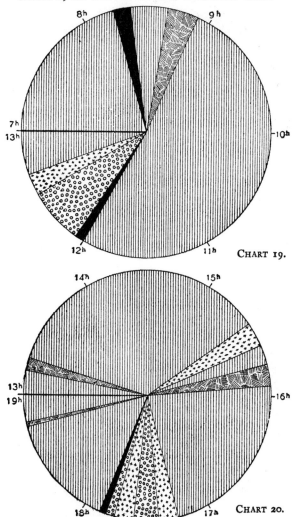

CHART 19.

CHART 20.

[1] For legend of Charts 19-30, see p. 146.

153

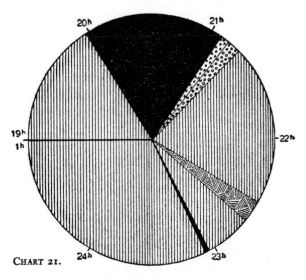

CHART 21.

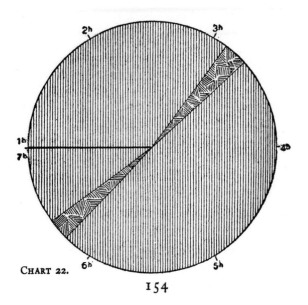

CHART 22.

Day Cycles and Developmental Progress

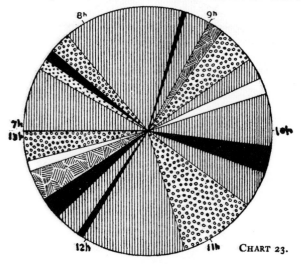

CHART 23.

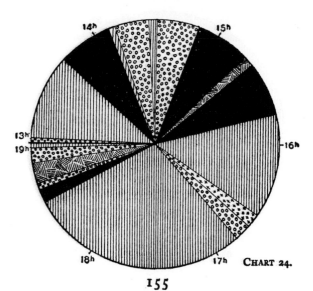

CHART 24.

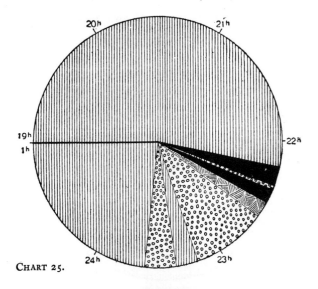

CHART 25.

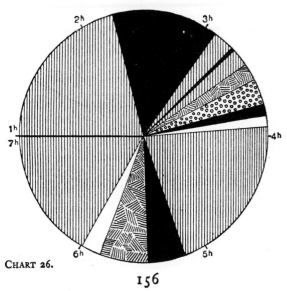

CHART 26.

Day Cycles and Developmental Progress

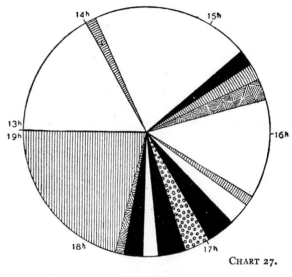

CHART 27.

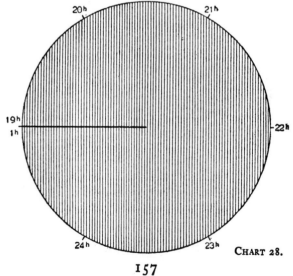

CHART 28.

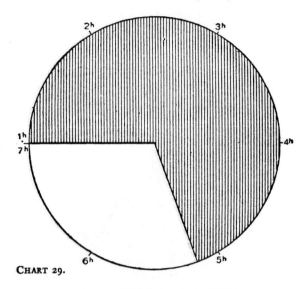

CHART 29.

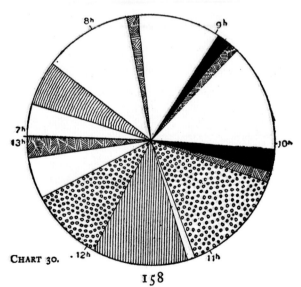

CHART 30.

Day Cycles and Developmental Progress

| Sleep | Taking Nourishment | Quiet Waking | Negative Reaction | Random Movements | Approaching and Experimentation |

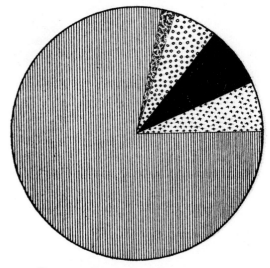

CHART 31. Day cycle of B 2:0; 0 (+4).

S	....	1,126'
N	....	25'
R	....	82' (D 82')
U	....	115'
B	....	92'
Total	....	1,440' = 24 hours

159

and found that the progress of development which we had ascertained by general observations were confirmed by individual cases. Let us discuss some of these cases with the aid of diagrams of individual days.

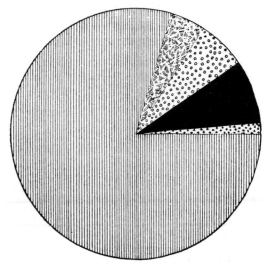

CHART 32. Day cycle of B 2:0; 1.

S .... 1,132′
N .... 66′
R .... 90′ (D 90′)
U .... 132′
B .... 20′

Total .... 1,440′ = 24 hours

B 2 was observed on the fourth day after birth and at the end of the first month. In his case, we see no decrease of the daily value for sleeping and dozing, but his waking state is divided each month in a different way. The positive reactions have increased in so far as the one month old child needs more time for the taking of food but the negative reactions have also become more numerous. We have already mentioned that the maximum day value for negative reaction is

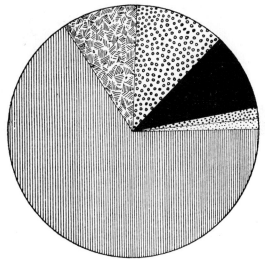

CHART 33. Day cycle of B 12:0; 2.

S	....	946′
N	....	141′ (P 8′ D 160′)
R	....	168′
U	....	144′
B	....	21′
Ex	....	20′
Total	....	1,440′ = 24 hours

established as occurring during the first month (Tables XXIV and XXV).

B 12 was observed by us at the ages of two and three months (charts 33 and 34). With the aid of the circles we can see the following development:

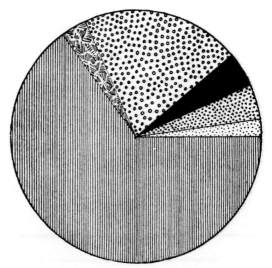

CHART 34. Day cycle of B 12:0; 3.

S .... 933′
N .... 48′ (P 90′ D 206′)
R .... 296′
U .... 66′
B .... 64′
Ex .... 33′
                        ─────
   Total .... 1,440′ = 24 hours

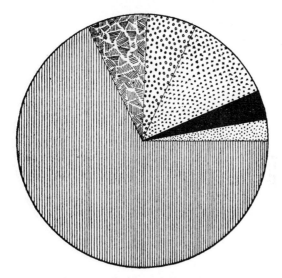

CHART 35. Day cycle of G 22:0; 4.

S	911'
N	113' (P 26' D 66')
R	92'
U	118'
B	166'
Ex	30'
Total	1,440' = 24 hours

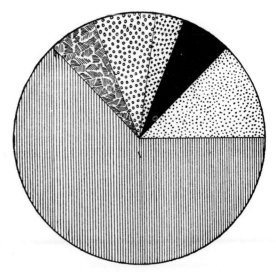

CHART 36. Day cycle of G 22:0; 5.

S .... 792′
N .... 90′
R .... 117′ (P 60′ D 57′)
U .... 94′
B .... 55′
Ex .... 292′
                        _____
   Total .... 1,440′ = 24 hours

Day Cycles and Developmental Progress

There now occur increase of the positive quiet waking state, of spontaneous reactions (aimless movements and experimenting), and decrease of approach-

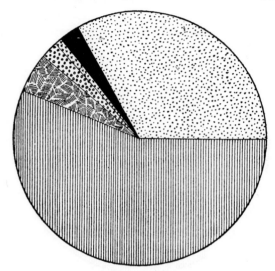

CHART 37. Day cycle of G 22:0; 6.

S	803′
N	75′
R	32′ (P 30′ D 2′)
U	38′
B	15′
Ex	477′
Total	1,440′ = 24 hours

ing movements when taking food and of negative reactions.

We observed G 22 three times, when she was four, five, and six months old. She shows the progress of development especially clearly since we could also watch her in just those months when the greatest progress toward spontaneity and the positive side is made. This explains the great increase of day values for experimenting, and the decrease of impulsive movements,

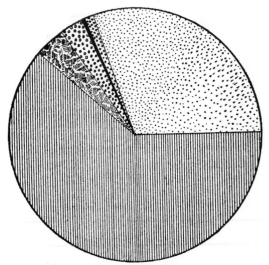

CHART 38. Day cycle of G 39:0; 8.

S	....	912′
N	....	58′
R	....	44′ (P 30′ D 14′)
U	....	5′
B	....	18′
Ex	....	403′
	Total	1,440′ = 24 hours

negative reactions, and the dozing state, and is another proof of growing spontaneity.

G 39, who could be watched when eight and eleven months old (charts 38 and 39), shows also the decrease of undirected actions (aimless movements) and of sleep, and also the growth of spontaneous behavior.

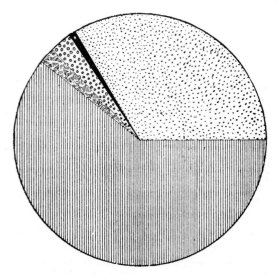

CHART 39. Day cycle of G 39:0; 11.

S	....	863′
N	....	31′
R	....	42′ (P 26′ D 16′)
U	....	16′
Ex	....	578′
Total	....	1,440′ = 24 hours

167

CHAPTER XII

The Stages of Development

EACH month of the first year of life brings to the child something new and essential. But not each month seems to be equally significant for his development. There are times in which a mass of newly appearing facts, a series of unexpected progresses in every phase, indicate that we are at a turning-point in the course of the child's development. They divide themselves into a number of periods which we shall have to characterize further.

The first turning-point lies between the second and third months. In all directions we can make new observations. The greatest decline of the curve indicating the day value of sleep is ended (Chapter X, Tables XVII and XVIII, chart 6). The maximum day value for negative reactions is passed (Chapter X, chart 11, Tables XXIV and XXV). Food is no longer received so greedily, so that now the child interrupts his sucking for seconds and opens his eyes. All conditions for activity beyond merely eating, sleeping, and crying, are present. The frequency of reactions to single stimuli has become small in comparison with that of the newborn (Chapter IX, Tables XV and XVI). Sleep-disturbances from within and the frightened shrinking in response to external sensory stimuli become considerably less frequent (Chapter VIII, chart 4). Continuous activities and actions therefore occur much more often (Chapter IX, chart 5). At this time new ways of behavior are added, such as playful experimenting, lalling, the first activity of the senses, the first active reaction to position, the first coördination of two organs acting simultaneously, the first social reactions, and expressional movements such as those of function pleasure and ill-humored astonishment (compare Chapters V and VI, and Appendix). All this indicates that the passivity with which the newborn met its surrounding has been succeeded by a receptive interest which is shown most clearly by the newly appearing receptive waking-state. Instead of the passivity from which the child was aroused only by strong sensory stimuli, we have now, as was said once before, the inclination to subject oneself to the stimulus. Here it occurs for the first time that the child pays attention to his own movements, his own sound-utterances, and to other human beings. The interest with which he meets all these now makes possible the further development in all other spheres.

An equally important turning-point lies between the fifth and sixth months. From then on, sleeping and waking take up equal parts of the day (Chapter X, Tables XVII and XVIII). The day value for neutral reactions experiences an enormous increase between the fourth and fifth month (Chapter X, chart 9), as does the day value for positive expressional movements. The change from a majority of single reactions and impulsive movements to a majority of continuous activities and actions is consummated during the fifth month (Chapter IX, chart 5, Tables XIV and XVI). At this time we observe new ways of behavior, such as the first certain movements of defense, the first sure grasping, the first lively outbursts of joy, crying when an intended movement does not succeed, and perhaps also the first desiring, experimentative actions, social reactions toward ·comrades, seeking for lost toys (Chapters V, VI, VII, and Appendix).

All these ways of behavior show a certain liveliness, an active seeking for stimuli, active participation which goes beyond reactions to stimuli, which become especially apparent in the growing day value for spontaneous reactions. These facts cannot be explained merely by the receptive interest alone. We may presume that it has now been succeeded by an active interest in the world.

An important turning-point appears at the tenth month, in which, after the disappearance of aimless movements during the ninth month, we find the first steps toward a further development of a higher kind (Chapter VI), the first use of tones and words expressing desire. With this the child enters into a new period, the conclusion of which is not reached during the first year.

INVENTORY OF THE OBSERVED BEHAVIORS

o ; o

1. Sleep

Position of fetus, impulsive movements and sounds, sucking movements in sleep.

Reaction to strong sensory stimuli, nourishment taken in sleep, disturbances from without, disturbances from within resulting or not resulting in awakening, convulsive movements, restlessness, eyes forcefully opened, crying out.

2. Transitional states
   (a) falling asleep
   (b) awakening

Convulsive movements.
Head thrown back, arms stretched out, slow opening of eyes.

   (c) state of fatigue

Eyes blank, expression of face relaxed, yawning. Eyes shut and forcefully opened, eyes half closed.

3. State of tranquil waking

   (a) dozing

Relaxed expression of face, blank eyes, immobility.

4. Taking in of food

Sucking when touched by stimulating object, arms pressed to body while taking in of food, fists clenched, swallowing, licking, accidental clucking sounds, taking food during sleep.

5. State of hunger and satiation

Ceasing of suckling movements; interrupted suckling movements; vomiting.

6. Movements expressing emotional states

   (a) greed

   ——

   (b) active displeasure

Restless, aimless, excited movements, with or without sound-utterance, grimacing of face.

   (c) fright

Convulsive movements, frightened sounds, contraction of body, frowns, arms and legs drawn up, eyes shut tight, fists clenched.

Convulsive movements, frightened sounds, head thrown back, arms and legs stretched out, fingers spread, eyes forcefully opened.

7. Reactions of flight and defense

Aimless movements, crying.

8. Aimless movements

Impulsive movements of head, limbs, lips, eyes squinted.

9. Reactions to position

   ——

10. Reactions to change of position

11. Reactions to perception

   ——

   (a) general reactions

Reflexes, fright, utterances of displeasure, interruption of movements and sounds, head turned away at strong sensory stimuli.

   (b) hearing

Head turned toward sounds.

   (c) seeing

Pupils widened, pupils narrowed, head turned toward lights, eyes resting on lightened fields.

   (d) touching

Grasping reflex.

12. Grasping

Grasping reflex.

Inventory of the Observed Behaviors

13. Experimenting in play ——
14. Thinking ——
15. Sound-utterings Crying, sounds of fright accidentally uttered, disconnected sounds.
16. Social reactions ——
17. Interest ——

o ; 1

ADDITIONAL REACTIONS.

1. Sleep As in o ; o ——
2. Transitional states
   (a) falling asleep " " " Utterance of some sounds, soft cries.
   (b) awakening " " " Restless movements of arms across face.
   (c) fatigue " " " ——
   (d) transition from excitement to quiet " " " Compare with "dozing."
3. Tranquil waking
   (a) dozing " " " ——
   (b) state of comfort " " " Tightening of facial muscles, eyes gleaming, corners of mouth drawn up.
4. Taking of nourishment " " " Head turned toward breast, mouth opened when spoon touches lips, smacking sounds.
5. State of hunger and satiation " " " Characteristic hunger-cries, continuous, loud, interrupted by sucking movements.
   Head drawn back, bottle nipple ejected, stretching of body.
6. Movements expressing emotional states
   (a) greed " " " ——
   (b) active displeasure " " " Tears, frowns, tight shutting of eyes, rubbing of face against pillow.
   (c) fright " " " ——
   (d) displeased astonishment " " " Eyes forcefully opened, mouth

172

Inventory of the Observed Behaviors

		opened, eyebrows drawn up, forehead taut, arms lifted.
(e) state of pleasure	As in o; o	Eyes gleaming, corners of mouth drawn up, eyes looking up.
7. Reactions of flight and defense	" " "	Head turned away, arms drawn up to face, arms stretched sideways.
8. Aimless movements	——	——
9. Reaction to position	——	——
10. Reaction to change of position	——.	——
11. Reactions to perception		
(a) general reactions	As in o; o	——
(b) hearing	" " "	Restlessness when hearing sounds.
(c) seeing	" " "	Staring, blinking.
(d) touching	" " "	——
12. Grasping	" " "	——
13. Experimenting at play	——	——
14. Thinking	——	——
15. Utterance of sounds	As in o; o	Sounds of pleasure, shrill cries, groaning, smacking sounds.
16. Social reactions	——	Crying when another child cries.
17. Interest	——	——

o; 2

1. Sleep	As in o; 1	——
2. Transition from sleeping to waking		
(a) falling asleep	" " "	——
(b) awakening	" " "	Violent turning of head, stretching of body and arms.
(c) fatigue	" " "	Lifting of heavy eyelids.
(d) transition from excitement to quiet	" " "	

Inventory of the Observed Behaviors

3. Tranquil waking
   (a) dozing — As in o; 1 — ——
   (b) state of comfort — " " " — ——
   (c) receptive waking
       state — —— — Eyes suddenly open and staring, taut features, slight frowns, lips pursed and pushed forward.

4. Taking in food — " " " — Eyes opened while taking in food, sucking interrupted at intervals for several seconds.

5. State of hunger and satiation — " " " — Mouth opened after removal of food if not sated.

6. Expressions of emotional states
   (a) greed — " " " — ——
   (b) active displeasure — " " " — Lips pressed together, head thrown back, body reared, eyes opened and shut.
   (c) fright — " " " — ——
   (d) displeased astonishment — — Fingers spread, arms stretched out.
   (e) state of comfort — " " " — Accompanying lalling sounds, some lusty movements.
   (f) surprise followed by interest — — ——
   (g) function pleasure — — Corners of mouth drawn up, eyes gleaming during movement and experimenting.

7. Reactions of flight and defense — " " " — Evading attack with part of body only.

8. Aimless movements — Some movements accompanied by function pleasure.

9. Reactions to position — Head held upright, head held up when lying on stomach.

10. Reactions to change of position — ——

11. Reactions to perception

174

Inventory of the Observed Behaviors

ADDITIONAL REACTIONS.

(a) general reactions	As in o; 1	Watching sense-perceptions. Other occupations interrupted by slight sensory stimuli.
(b) hearing	" " "	Head turns searchingly while sound lasts, eyes twitch at strong noises.
(c) seeing	" " "	Objects fixated, the face turned toward constantly lighted fields, objects followed with eyes and turning of head. Eyes grow cross-eyed after prolonged gazing.
(d) touching	" " "	Active touching, blinking when touching.
(e) coördination		Coördinating of auditory impressions and self-produced sounds.
12. Grasping	" " "	Touching objects, grasping for tactually perceived objects.

13. Experimenting in play
    (a) on own body

        I. Continuous activity, bending and stretching of limbs, fingers, tongue.

        Lifting and lowering of limbs, turning of head, arms, legs, hands and fingers in their joints.

        II. Opening and shutting of eyes and mouth.

        III. Movements in one direction and back again.

        IV. Touching, pressing, rubbing and beating of several parts of the body against others.

        V. Hands put into mouth or one into the other.

    (b) on objects   I. Continuous experimental activity.

        II. Handling of static objects. Touching of objects.

14. Thinking   ———

15. Vocalizations   " " "   Lalling, habitual crying, sounds of astonishment, repetition of

Inventory of the Observed Behaviors

own sounds, sighing, groaning, sobbing, soft whimpering, sounds of effort and of enjoyment during movement.

16. Social relations
    (a) to grownups

Answering looks with laughter, getting disquieted by approach and by talking, crying when grownup who is occupied with child leaves it.

    (b) to comrades   As in o; 1
17. Interest shown   Receptive waking state.

o; 3

1. Sleep   As in o; 2
2. Transitional states   " " "
3. Tranquil waking   " " "
4. Taking in of food   " " "
5. State of hunger and satiation   " " "   Aimless movements toward bottle, spitting.

6. Movements expressing emotional states
    (a) greed   " " "
    (b) active displeasure   " " "
    (c) fright   " " "
    (d) displeased astonishment   " " "
    (e) state of comfort   " " "   Stretching out of tongue.
    (f) functions   " " "
    (g) interested surprise   " " "
7. Reactions of flight and defense   " " "
8. Aimless movements   " " "
9. Reaction to position   " " "   Head and shoulders held high, when lying on stomach.

10. Reaction to change of position   " " "
11. Reaction to perception
    (a) general reaction   " " "   Happy sounds at reception of sense impressions.

176

ADDITIONAL REACTIONS.

(b) hearing	As in o; 2	Active hearing.
(c) seeing	" " "	Eyes seeking source of sound.
(d) touching	" " "	Looking around.
(e) coördination	" " "	Eyes searching for object of sound.
12. Grasping	" " "	Eyes following own movements.
13. Playful experimenting		
(a) on own body	" " "	Bending and stretching neck, lifting and lowering head, grasping one hand with other and moving it. Accompanying sounds of lalling.
(b) on objects	" " "	Accompanying sounds of lalling.
14. Thinking		——
15. Vocalizations	" " "	Lalling as accompaniment of experimenting.
16. Social reactions		
(a) to grownups	" " "	Laughing at grownup, stretching out tongue, disquieted by approach, answering look of approaching person with lalling.
(b) to comrade	" " "	
17. Interest		——

o; 4

1. Sleep	As in o; 3	Other sleeping positions besides the fetal.
2. Transitional states		
(a) falling asleep	" " "	Body turned sideways, stretching.
(b) awakening	" " "	
(c) fatigue	" " "	Slowing up of movements.
(d) transition from excitement to quiet		
3. Tranquil waking state	" " "	
4. Taking in of nourishment	" " "	Biting of objects, disquiet caused by approach of bottle,

177

ADDITIONAL REACTIONS.

mouth opened at coming of spoon, hands tightened around bottle, social laughter, sounds of comfort interrupting sucking, bottle pushed away with the head.

5. State of satiation — As in o; 3 — Shaking of head.

6. Expressions of emotional states — " " "

7. Reactions of flight and defense — " " "

Along with the movement of flight the limbs move toward stimulus, bottle is pushed away with head.

8. Aimless movements — " " "

9. Reactions to position — " " "

10. Reactions to change of position — " " "

Attempt to push body sideways and forward, and to turn when lying on stomach.

11. Reaction to perception — " " "

   (a) general reactions — " " "

   (b) hearing — " " "

   (c) seeing — " " "

Regarding object of touch, active watching.

   (d) touching — " " "

   (e) coördinations — " " "

Grasping for perceived objects that are brought nearer.

12. Grasping — " " "

Both hands grasping at the same time without using fingers (fists). Both hands clasping object at same time using palms.

13. Playful experimenting

   (a) on own body — " " "

   (b) on objects — " " "

Handling and moving of objects. Grasping, holding and moving, raising and lowering and shaking of objects.

14. Thinking — ——

15. Vocalization — As in o; 3 — Eyes widely opened when crying.

Inventory of the Observed Behaviors

ADDITIONAL REACTIONS.

16. Social reactions
    (a) to grownup   As in o; 3   Ill-humor when person, once seen, goes away again. Caresses comforting.

    (b) to playmate   ——
17. Interest   As in o; 3
18. Desire   Impatient struggling after unsuccessful posture-reactions.

o; 5

1. Sleep   As in o; 4
2. Transitional states
    (a) falling asleep   " " "
    (b) awakening   " " "   Rubbing eyes.
    (c) fatigue   " " "
    (d) from excitement
        to quiet   " " "
3. Tranquil waking   " " "
4. Taking in food   " " "   Bottle-stopper pushed into mouth, attention for surroundings while sucking.

5. State of hunger and
    satiation   " " "
6. Expressions of emotional states
    (a-g)   " " "
    (h) joy   Lively moving of arms and legs, eyes gleaming, corners of mouth drawn up, joy-sounds, mouth forcefully opened.

7. Reactions of flight
    and defense   " " "   Definite defense-movements, pushing away of stimulus.
8. Aimless movements   " " "
9. Reactions to position   " " "   Supporting body on hands when lying on stomach.

10. Reactions to change
    of position   " " "   When lying on back, head and shoulders lifted, attempt made to sit up with aid of hands, turning from back to side.

11. Reactions to perception   " " "

179

Inventory of the Observed Behaviors

12. Grasping   As in o; 4   Fingers used as both hands grasp for object simultaneously, hands also grasp singly for objects.

13. Playful experimenting
    (a) on own body   " " "   I. Experimenting on possible reactions to changes of position.
    (b) on objects   " " "   II. Experimentive actions: beating an object, pulling on it, drawing it nearer.

14. Thinking   ———
15. Vocalization   " " "   Constant sounds of ill-humor, joy, surprise.

16. Social reactions
    (a) to grownup   " " "   Sight of person upsetting, play interrupted while he is visible. Attacking person, increased crying when he approaches.
    (b) to comrade   " " "   Observing another child, laughing at it.

17. Interest   Active interest.
18. Desire   " " "   Looking at desired object, desirous sounds, ill-humor.

o; 6

1. Sleep   As in o; 5
2. Transitional states
    (a) going to sleep   " " "   Rubbing eyes.
    (b) awakening   " " "
3. Quiet waking   " " "
4. Taking in food   " " "   Chewing.
5. State of satiation   " " "   Bottle pushed away, stretching, beating at bottle.

6. Emotional states
    (a-g)   " " "
    (h) joy   " " "   Laughing as a general reaction, clapping hands, crowing, smacking, spreading of fingers.

7. Reaction of flight and defense   " " "   Defensive holding to object.
8. Aimless movement   " " "
9. Reaction to position   " " "   Sitting up when supported.

180

Inventory of the Observed Behaviors

10. Reactions to changed
    position   As in o; 5   Turning from stomach to back, drawing body foreward sideways.

11. Reactions to perception
    (a-d)   " " "
    (e)   " " "   Coördination of own movement and own sounds.

12. Grasping   " " "   Grasping with feet, hand, and foot simultaneously, bringing seized objects up to mouth, grasping all objects that have been perceived.

13. Playful experimenting
    (a) on own body   " " "   Laughing accompanies experiment.
    (b) on objects   " " "   Pushing away, lifting, putting away, and allowing objects to drop.

14. Thinking
15. Vocalization   " " "   Crowing.
16. Social reactions
    (a) to grownup   " " "   Arousing attention of grownup by lalling, answering words of grownup by lalling, stretching hands toward grownup, crying when he ceases to speak.
    (b) to comrade   " " "
17. Interest   " " "
18. Desire   " " "

                   o; 7

1. Sleep   As in o; 6   Sounds, impulsive movements rare; sleeping reception of food ceases.

2. Transitional states   " " "
3. Tranquil waking   " " "
    (a) dozing   " " "
    (b) state of comfort   " " "
    (c) receptive waking   " " "
    (d) contemplative
        waking   Eyes tightly shut, features

Inventory of the Observed Behaviors

taut, lips pushed forward, mouth pursed.

4. Taking in food   As in o ; 6   Suckling movements caused by stimulation of object touching lips now cease. Food held and bitten into.

5. State of satiation   " " "
6. Emotional states
    (a-h)   " " "
    (i) quiet ill-humor   Eyes gleamless, corners of mouth drop.

7. Reaction of flight
    and defense   " " "   Feet push away objects.
8. Aimless movements   " " "
9. Reaction to position   " " "   Attempt to crawl forward.
10. Reaction to changed
    position   " " "
11. Reactions to obser-
    vations   " " "
12. Grasping   " " "   Grasping, with simultaneous change of position.

13. Playful experiment-
    ing
    (a) on own body   " " "
    (b) on objects   " " "   Turning and tearing objects, using one object on another static one, knocking one against the other.

14. Thinking
15. Vocalization   " " "   Shouting with joy, pleased cries, squeaking.
16. Social reactions   " " "   Quieting down when kindly spoken to.
17. Interest   " " "
18. Desire   " " "   Desire to reach objects through change of position.

o; 8

1. Sleep   As in o; 7
2. Transition from
    sleeping to waking   " " "
3. Quiet waking
    (a-d)   " " "

Inventory of the Observed Behaviors

(e) state of discom-
fort

              Eyes gleamless, corners of mouth drop.

4. Taking in food   As in o ; 7   Preparations for feeding become quieter.

5. State of satiation   " " "

6. Emotional expressions
    (a-i)   " " "
    (k) depression   Soft crying.
    (l) fear   Loud crying, movements of flight and defense.

    (m) strong expectation and joyous astonishment   Followed by expressions of joy.

7. Reactions of flight and defense   " " "   Flight with whole body.

8. Aimless movements   " " "

9. Reaction to position   " " "   Lying supported by one hand when on stomach, sitting up freely.

10. Reaction of changed position   " " "   Straightening to sitting position with support.

11. Use of senses   " " "

12. Grasping   " " "

13. Playful experimenting
    (a) on own body   " " "
    (b) on objects   " " "   Putting one object into another (beginning of construction), handling two moving objects, rubbing and knocking objects against each other.

14. Thinking

15. Utterances   " " "

16. Social reactions   " " "

17. Interest   " " "

18. Desire   " " "

              o ; 9

1-7.   As in o ; 8

8. Aimless movements   Impulsive movements disappear.

Inventory of the Observed Behaviors

9. Reaction to position	As in o; 8		Standing and kneeling when supported.
10. Reaction to changed position	" " "		Sitting up without support.
11-12.	" " "		
13. Playful experimenting			
(a) on own body	" " "		
(b) on objects	" " "		Scratching surface of objects, separating parts, throwing objects.
14. Thinking	" " "		Forming false mechanical connections.
15. Vocalizations	" " "		Habitual crying disappears.
16. Social reactions			
(a) to grownup	" " "		Arousing attention through movements, pulling dress of grownup to attract her.
(b) to comrade	" " "		Crying when another child is watched, holding out toy to another child, lalling at it.
17-18.	" " "		

o; 10

1-12.	As in o; 9		
13. Playful experimenting			
(a) on own body	" " "		Organized play-activity on own body.
(b) on objects	" " "		Standing up objects, taking one out of another, drawing them close with a cord, pushing an object back and forth with another.
14. Thinking			Tool thinking, fetching object by means of cord.
15. Vocalizations	" " "		Words of desire.
16. Social reactions			
(a) to grownup	" " "		Reaching objects to him, lalling, imitating his dealing with a toy.
(b) to comrade	" " "		Imitating movements of an-

184

Inventory of the Observed Behaviors

other child, defense against taking away toys.

17-18.　　　　　　　As in o; 9

　　　　　　　　　　　　　　　o; 11

1-9.　　　　　　　　As in o; 10
**10. Reaction to changed
　　　position**　　　　" " "　　　　Standing up with support.
11-12.　　　　　　　" " "
**13. Playful experiment-
　　　ing**
　　　(a) on own body　　" " "
　　　(b) on objects　　　　　　　　　Standing up objects.
14-15.　　　　　　　" " "
16. Social reactions
　　　(a) to grownup　　" " "　　　　Organized social play-activity.
　　　(b) to comrade　　" " "　　　　Organized social play-activity,
arousing attention of another
child through lalling, signs of
ill-humor when child leaves,
putting aside toys and turning
to another child.
17-18.　　　　　　　" " "

　　　　　　　　　　　　　　　1; 0

1-9.　　　　　　　　As in o; 11
**10. Reaction to changed
　　　position**　　　　　　　　　　Walking with support.
11-12.　　　　　　　" " "
**13. Playful experiment-
　　　ing**
　　　(a) on own body　　" " "
　　　(b) on objects　　　" " "　　　Pushing one object back and
forth with another.
14-15.
16. Social reactions
　　　(a) to grownup　　" " "　　　　When frightened or surprised,
looking at grownup.
　　　(b) to comrade　　" " "
17-18.　　　　　　　" " "

PART II

THE TESTS FOR THE FIRST AND SECOND
YEAR OF LIFE

CHAPTER I

Introduction to the Baby Tests

THE series of tests reported upon in this investigation makes it possible for the first time to determine by simple method the stage of development of children at the earliest age-levels. Heretofore, the youngest children to be included in any test series have been three-year-olds. For children below this age only single performances were known, which isolated findings indicated little, and could lead to no conclusive judgments of the child's developmental attainment. The new principle in our work, however, is not to be found in the early age of two and three months at which we begin testing, but in the procedure of choosing and collecting the test assignments.

Binet was the first to undertake to determine the mental plane of a child—and in his case it was a question of differentiating the feeble-minded children from the normal by means of performances. For the purpose of accomplishing this in as short a time as possible, with an easily administrable method, he set up in a purely instinctive fashion a series of performances which, according to his opinion, showed the degree of the child's intelligence at a certain age. By trying out these tests on a large number of children, he arrived statistically at a fixed assignment of the individual tests to certain age-levels—and to his concept of mental age. This concept has remained a basic idea in test methodology.

The First Year of Life

It is not our purpose here to enter at length into the discussions which have developed in connection with Binet's undertaking; we wish to raise only certain points of criticism which bring out the basic concept of our scheme of testing. A first and familiar occasion for criticism was the fact that Binet's tests were all to be given through the medium of language and all demanded performances largely language-conditioned. The practical sense of the Americans sought to overcome this objection by creating non-language tests. One of the first systems of this kind was prepared by Pintner and Paterson with emphasis upon the use of form-boards—i.e., constructive work. Other series were systematically directed at the perception of relations on concrete material—as, for instance, the Princeton tests, which are in part excellent. In all of these the basic principle of the Binet system is retained—namely, that one can determine the mental level of an individual and the degree of mental development of a child by means of a series of assignments, the performance of which calls for intellectual abilities in some more or less distinct way. The excellent Stanford revision of the Binet tests, as well as the clever tests devised by such men as Thorndike, Terman, Yerkes, and other outstanding psychologists, present only an ultimate improvement and expansion along this given direction.

But, as Thorndike and other leaders in this field ask: What is it that we are testing? What are we measuring? What traits do our tests apprehend? As a matter of fact, this question has become increasingly pressing. Despite Stern's endeavor to analyze more closely the concept of intelligence involved herein; despite the more exact attempts of the most modern

performance methods to deal with the conception of
relations, the essence of the thinking process; despite
Lippman-Bogen's attempt to do justice to the intelligence of practical life as well as of theory—despite all
these efforts, no one has been spared the vexing feeling of not really knowing what relative importance the
concrete prescribed performance, if carried out, merits
with respect to the total complex of mental abilities,
nor how the ability responsible for this performance
should rank in determining the mental plane of an individual. For what is indicated by the fact that a person does or does not grasp the relation between two
ideas or two wooden figures? Does that inform us in
any way whether he thinks and acts independently
or dependently; whether he has intellectual problems
or is mentally dull?—let alone the important facts of
endurance, of interest and direction of interests, and
all the character traits which go to make up the plane
of a person and which are not even touched upon? At
this point it is essential to pause and to ask just what
one should demand of a series of tests.

If one wants, as Binet did originally, nothing more
than a means of differentiating subnormal from normal
children through an approximate picture of their deviation from the normal average thinking of others of
their age, there are no objections to be made to the
customary method. It is different, however, when one
undertakes to say something *positive* and absolute
about the plane of a person and to alter the course of
his life, or, where possible, predict a future genius on
the basis of a few tests. As if the very essence of a productive mind were not to create independently and un-
influenced by prescribed assignments and goals! Using
the customary test to this end, constitutes quite simply

a misuse. A method which distinguishes the *sub*normal from the normal is far from being a method of seeking out the *super*normal as well, in as much as productivity, which is the ability to be considered here as worthy of fostering rather than facility of learning, is something qualitatively altogether different from that which is dealt with in the test assignments of such series.

In what does this difference consist? First, in the fact that productivity, as stated above, does not occur along prescribed lines, but as a free elaboration of that which has been acquired by learning and experience or by maturation. Productivity can never be measured by a definite limited task with a prescribed goal. If mental talents are to be tested, mental freedom must be assured. In this age of uninterrupted talk about the freedom of the child in work and play and regard for individual differences, this statement should hardly have to be made for the first time. In addition to our demand that tests, desiring to determine the individual's level positively rather than merely its relative deviation, should permit of a certain free play in the performance of their assignments, we must also, and above all, demand that they actually test the level and not simply intellectual dexterity, maturity, or even ability. The ability to think is not everything—nor yet the ability to learn. Truisms as these may be today, they are still apparently undiscovered as far as testing is concerned. Accordingly, test items must be so altered basicly as to measure the individual in all the varied aspects of his life.

If we ask ourselves how these theoretically recognized demands can be realized in practice, we find the answer in fitting our tests more closely to the natural

course of life and the natural determiners of performances. This means that tests, in order to fulfill the desired requirements, must be conscientiously based upon
an exact knowledge of the necessity and possibility of
performances in the stage of development to be considered. In this connection, the important point is not
that the test measures anything a child could do if need
be, but that it measures just exactly that which is characteristic of one stage of development and maturation,
or what distinguishes one level from another. Not any
random performance is needed, but just that one which
designates a step in the development and a stage of
maturity. Arnold Gesell was the first person to plan
his tests along these lines; it is his merit to have broken
away in practice from the old concept even though he
did not theoretically formulate tests based on a different principle. He starts with the systematic observation of the total behavior of children and tests their
developmental age by having them perform assignments in which typical steps of maturation are brought
out. His work has not yet been carried through to
quantitative standardization.

Stimulated to a great extent by the practice and procedure of Gesell, but with a view to a quantitative
evaluation from the very beginning, we built up our
test system. In doing so our interest has not been re-
stricted to the child's intelligence but has been directed
at his personality as a whole. We wished to determine
the stage of his development in the mastery of life.
The theoretical basis for the various dimensions to be
found in the mastery of life is supplied by the two following considerations: (1) We depend in our mastery
of life on our whole psycho-physical system, so that
physical as well as mental control of the situation must

be taken into account. (2) Our lives are concerned with man and materials—which is to say, we live among people and we work with materials. Life requires that we master both situations—social life and work, these situations being to a certain extent interdependent. With this as a point of departure, our main viewpoints are: How does the child develop in *physical* and *mental* control of himself and the situation, and how does he develop in *social relationships* and in the *manipulation of materials?*

Our tests are constructed to measure the single activities which combine to form the main lines of action. Our greatest security lies in the fact that we arrive at the stage of maturity and determine the level of the individual by approaching the total system of action and not single intellectual functions. For a basis the inventory of behavior for the first year of age was used, as well as a number of special investigations which give a comprehensive picture of this period, more complicated than all others in its structure. The theoretical bases for the separate tests are therefore to be found in the special investigations based upon the general presentation of Charlotte Bühler and will not be discussed here. We shall only show, in short, how the action-system of the age with which we are occupied is examined in its different dimensions.

CHAPTER II

Instructions for Giving the Tests

EACH test in the following series is designated by a letter, according to which of the four main lines of action it belongs. B stands for bodily control, M for mental ability, S for social development, O for manipulation of objects.

We have described after each test the reaction which must take place if the item is to be considered passed. We mark this +.

For the sake of brevity we have kept to the terminology already used in the inventory and in the practical studies which have been made in connection with it. For a thorough understanding of the tests, a knowledge of these studies is essential; the significance of the single test items can be grasped only in the light of their interrelationships, their psychological coherence. It is for the purpose of pointing to this that the brief test explanations have been included at the end of each series.

Each child is given a team of five test series: the one corresponding to his chronological age, the next two lower series and the next two higher series. For example, a six months old child is given series IV, V, VI, VII, and VIII [1]; a child aged 1;3 is given XI, 2-I, 2-II, 2-III, and 2-IV. Exceptions in this procedure will have to be made at the youngest end of the

[1] Test series are designated by Roman numerals (in the second year 2-I, 2-II, etc.) ; test items by Arabic.

scale, in as much as the series do not go below two months; and at the older end of the scale approaching two years, the test series beyond this point having not as yet been standardized. Alterations in this team of tests can be left to the discretion of the examiner [2] in those cases where consistent failure in one series shows the presentation of a higher series to be unnecessary, or where consistent passing in one series makes presentation of a lower series unnecessary.

The test items should not be presented to the child in a mechanical way. An examination is possible only if the child is in the proper condition. In the case of tiring or continued negative reactions it is advisable to interrupt the testing and continue another time. With children of eight months or older the examiner should occupy herself for a while before beginning the test in order to avoid giving the disturbing impression of strangeness. Younger children are wearied by such attentions beforehand, so that with them it is better to start right in with the testing. The order of the test items should not be strictly adhered to. Some reactions cannot be evoked by a single test situation; in such a case, a casual observation may prove a substitute. According to our experience there are always opportunities for such during the testing period, as all the test items are concerned with reactions so characteristic for the child at each respective age-level that they are bound to appear sooner or later. Questions asked of the child's parent or nurse may throw light on certain items. Often a single item can show whether the child is capable of performing others. For example, if, upon bringing an object to the hand of the four months old child, it reaches for the felt object, moves it about and

[2] Hereafter termed Ex.

fastens his glance upon it, one may consider the following items passed: grasping an object presented to touch, moving an object about and looking at it. In general, it is wise to begin with tests which may be expected to result in positive affective reactions, such as returning the glance with cooing or smiling; and to place tests with negative reactions at the end of the series, in order not to risk failures due to a change of mood.

Imitation is the hardest performance to score. We have never demanded of the child a precise repetition of the demonstrated movement. The performance was counted as passed if the child succeeded in bringing about an approximately similar movement with a show of exertion and effort.

It is to be noted that all articles of clothing which inhibit the child's movements should be removed.

SCORING

To begin with, a basal score is taken amounting to the number of completed months in the child's age [3] —that is:

For all children of age between 0; 2 and 0; 2 (+ 30), basal score = 0; 2.

For all children of age between 0; 3 and 0; 3 (+ 30), basal score = 0; 3.

In the second year the basal score is that of the completed age group—that is:

[3] The accepted form for stating ages is used throughout: the number of completed years before the semi-colon, the number of completed months after it, and the number of additional days affixed within parentheses, with a plus sign. For example:

0; 2 (+ 17) stands for an age of 2 months and 17 days.
3; 6 (+ 2) " " " " " 3 years, 6 months, and 2 days.

For all children of age between 1;0 and 1;2 (+ 30), basal
score = 1;0.

For all children of age between 1;3 and 1;5 (+ 30), basal
score = 1;3.

For all children of age between 1;6 and 1;9 (+ 30), basal
score = 1;6.

For all children of age between 1;9 and 1;11 (+ 30), basal
score = 1;9.

For every test item passed in the series of the child's own month and of the two older months, three days are added to the score. This evaluation results from the consideration of the fact that a hypothetically normal child of 0;2 might be unable to accomplish any item of the two months series, but would be able to perform them all at the age of 0;2 (+ 30). If we assume that this development takes a regular course, there being ten items and thirty days, we can conclude that the child learns to accomplish one item in three days. The ideal child of 0;2 (+ 10) would then be able to fulfill 10/30 of the month's series; the child of 0;2 (+ 20) would fulfill 20/30; and the child of 0;2 (+ 30) would fulfill the whole series. Corresponding to these positive scores for items passed, there are negative scores for the failed performances in the series for the two months preceding the child's chronological age. For each of these, three days are subtracted from the score. In scoring the tests passed in the *second year series,* nine days is added to the score for each item, in as much as three months are now allowed for learning the respective ten items. Accordingly, nine days are subtracted from the score for each failure below the chronological level.

When it is doubtful whether or not a test has been passed, the test is not scored either way. It must be noted that several items will not be performed if the child is capable of higher accomplishments. In all such cases the performances of the lower levels should receive full credit.

An example of the scoring method taken from the case of B 486—chronological age 0; 5—follows:[4]

	0 ; 3	0 ; 4	0 ; 5	0 ; 6	0 ; 7
1	+	+	+	—	—
2	+	—	—	—	—
3	+	+	+	+	—
4	+	+	+	+	—
5	+	+	+	—	+
6	+	+	+	—	+
7	+	+	+	—	—
8	+	+	+	+	+
9	+	—	+	—	—
10	+	+	+	—	—
Failed	0	2	Passed 9	3	3
Total *F:*—2		Total *P:*—15			

D. A.-0 ; 5 — 2 (3 days) + 15 (3 days)-0 ; 6 + 9
D. Q.-126

THE DEVELOPMENTAL PROFILE

The inability of the final computation of the developmental age to convey an adequate picture of the child's personality and mentality is obvious. At best it gives the average attainment level.

[4] In addition to the accepted abbreviation C.A. for chronological age, D.A. is used for *developmental age,* and D.Q. for *developmental quotient.*

It is equally important and perhaps of even greater interest for the psychologist or parent to know the *distribution* of the child's abilities. This knowledge is, of course, obtainable on the basis of analysis of the test results. But, in order that some part of it may be graphically represented along with the test scoring, the record blanks include a "developmental profile." This is constructed to show the distribution of the child's abilities with respect to the aforementioned four major classifications of social reactions, bodily control, mental abilities, and the manipulation of objects. The four ordinates are designated, as the individual test items were, by the letters S, B, M, and O, respectively.

A table containing the credits to be used in connection with the profile is also included on each record blank. The values listed therein were obtained according to the following method. As in scoring the tests, negative values were assigned to failures below the chronological age, and positive values to performances above the basal age. The base in the profile is also taken as the number of completed months for cases falling within the first year, and the completed age-group for those within the second year. Negative and positive values are plotted with respect to the line representing this basal age. The method of calculating the numerical value in days can be shown by an example. In order to find the rating for mental tests, let us say, in the fourth month, the four M test items in series IV were considered separately, apart from the remaining items. According to the same procedure employed in calculating the scoring, the thirty days of the month were divided by the four items with the resulting credit of 7.5 for each mental test of series IV.

We may illustrate the procedure of plotting the developmental profile with the test results of B 486 which are shown in the scoring table.

Item	Series	No. failed	No. passed	Credits	Total
S	V	0	1	30	30
B	V		3	22.5	
	VI		2	20	
	VII		1	7.5	50
M	IV	1		−7.5	
	V		4	30	
	VI		1	7.5	
	VII		1	15	45
0	V		1	30	30

Plotting the figures found in the total column gives the following graph:

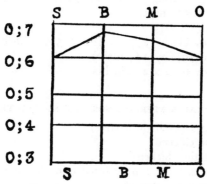

Developmental Profile B 486

LIST OF NECESSARY MATERIALS FOR TEST SERIES
I AND II

stop watch
screen
table
piece of cotton or gauze

zwieback
stiff paper
rattler
rattle
shiny object (a wooden disc 3½ inches in diameter covered with tin foil)
shrill whistle
animal mask
color-card (piece of cardboard covered with shiny colored paper)
figure-card (color-card with figures of vari-colored paper pasted on it)
flash-light (3 volt)
metal bell
rubber doll—(squeaks when squeezed)
2 other toys (small wooden or cloth animals or some such toy)
piece of white writing paper 6 x 8 inches
hand mirror 6 x 8 inches
picture book
nest of hollow blocks, 1½, 2, 2½, 3, 3½, 4 inches
plate of glass 19½ x 11¾ inches
cardboard box 6 x 4 x 2½ inches
rubber ball

ADDITIONAL MATERIALS FOR THE SECOND YEAR TESTS

2 wooden eggs (or little barrels)
ball with the chicken
ball without the chicken
2 hollow sticks (that can be fitted into one another)
drum with 2 drum sticks
box containing 6 wooden blocks
1 small red box } the same shape and size
1 small blue box }
spinning top
music box   } of cardboard, the pictures approximately
nonsense picture } the same size, coloration, and form ele-
picture of a nurse } ments

CHAPTER III

The Tests for the First Year of Life[1]

OUR tests were drawn up after making ten preliminary trials for each month and were then
given to thirty children in each month, making a
total of 400 children.[2] At the preliminary trials the
behavior of the child was recorded extensively in all
details. Such great agreement in the reactions of the
individual children was found that it was deemed unnecessary to carry out this exact notation in the main
series where the tests were recorded only as passed or
failed. The criteria for this will be given with the description of the single tests. This similarity of reactions may also be taken as evidence of the fact that
we investigated only the characteristic reactions of
each age-group. The appropriate choice of tests is
thereby likewise corroborated. Still a further proof is
given in a statistical check below. At this point we shall
give an exact description of the test series.

An examiner (Ex.) and an observer were at every
presentation of the tests, the examiner to carry out the
test situations with the child and the observer to record the results. The series of tests for each month
contains ten items, which are as follows:

[1] Our subjects were children in the *Kinderübernahmsstelle,* Vienna,
IX.

[2] The figures used in the translated edition have been supplemented
by more recently acquired data, and differ therefore from those found
in the original.

The First Year of Life

II Months.[3]

S   1. Response to adult's glance.
B   2. Holding the head erect.
B   3. Holding the head up in the prone position.
B   4. Head movement of flight.
M   5. Fright at a loud sound.
M   6. Searching head movements during prolonged sound.
M   7. Focusing on an object.
M   8. Reaction to changing tone of voice.
O   9. Cooing.
O   10. Experimenting movements.

III Months.

S   1. Returning the glance with smiling or cooing.
B   2. Holding the head and shoulders erect in the prone position.
B   3. Flight movements of the whole body in response to tactile stimulation.
M   4. Looking for the source of a sound.
M   5. Following moving objects with the eyes.
M   6. Changed reaction upon repeating the presentation of an auditory stimulus.
M   7. Reaction to the disappearance of the human face.
M   8. Mask test.
M   9. Imitating facial movements.
O   10. Feeling of objects (active touch).

IV Months.

S   1. Expression of displeasure when adult stops playing with the child.
B   2. Lying supported only by the palms of the hands.
B   3. Grasping with both hands without using the fingers.
B   4. Grasping a touched object.
B   5. Diaper experiment in lying position.
M   6. Active looking about in a new situation.

---

[3] Roman numerals designate the month; Arabic the test item.

M   7. Positive reaction to light.
M   8. Looking at an object while moving it.
M   9. Imitating facial expressions.
O   10. Manipulatory movement of an object.

V Months.

S   1. Reflecting friendly and angry facial expressions.
B   2. Holding the head and shoulders high in the dorsal position.
B   3. Turning from back to side and back again.
B   4. Grasping an object in view with one hand.
B   5. Diaper experiment in dorsal position.
M   6. Positive reaction to sounds.
M   7. Reaction to the withdrawal of a toy.
M   8. Looking for a lost toy.
M   9. Imitating facial expressions.
O   10. Defense reaction to the withdrawal of a toy.

VI Months.

S   1. Actively seeking contact.
S   2. Distinguishing between friendly and angry talking.
B   3. Sitting with support.
B   4. Diaper experiment in prone position.
B   5. Table-edge test.
M   6. Displeasure at unsuccessful grasping.
M   7. Smiling as a general reaction.
M   8. Expectation in response to the repetition of a stimulus.
M   9. Imitating sounds.
O   10. Manipulation on a stationary object with a moving object.

VII Months.

S   1. Distinguishes between angry and friendly facial expressions.
B   2. Locomotion.
B   3. Diaper experiment in the supported sitting position.

B   4. Moving toward a desired object by changing the position.

B   5. Pushing away a stimulus.

M   6. Loss of interest in a repeated stimulus.

M   7. Imitating knocking.

O   8. Taking a toy away from an adult.

O   9. The paper test.

O   10. Manipulating and moving two objects.

VIII Months.

B   1. Sitting alone.

B   2. Crawling.

B   3. Reaching for an object outside the crib.

M   4. Neutral reaction to single stimulus.

M   5. The mirror test.

M   6. Reaction to strange surroundings.

M   7. Imitating squeezing the doll.

M   8. Persisting reaction to withdrawal of toy.

M   9. Deliberate choice of toy.

O   10. Preferring paper to other objects.

IX Months.

S   1. Becoming accustomed to a strange adult.

S   2. Arousing an adult's attention.

S   3. Understanding gestures.

S   4. Playing cuckoo.

B   5. Kneeling with support.

B   6. Grasping two objects while sitting alone.

M   7. Curiosity for that which is hidden.

M   8. Imitating opening and shutting the picture book.

M   9. The pocket test.

O   10. "Destructive" activity.

X Months.

S   1. Turning in astonishment to an adult.

S   2. Organized play with an adult.

B   3. Standing with support.
B   4. The diaper experiment while sitting alone.
B   5. Throwing objects.
M   6. The glass plate test.
M   7. Imitating ringing the bell.
M   8. Memory test.
M   9. Uncovering a covered object.
O   10. Opening a box.

XI Months.

S   1. Organized play with an adult.
B   2. Rising to the sitting position.
M   3. Memory test.
M   4. Imitating beating two spoons together.
M   5. Imitating sounds.
M   6. Fear of the unfamiliar.
M   7. Pulling an object by its string.
O   8. Careful handling of a block.
O   9. Fitting hollow blocks into one another.
O   10. Opening a box.

II—TEST SERIES FOR THE TWO MONTHS OLD CHILD

In all situations where no other directions are given, the child lies on his back in his crib. In case the Ex. is not supposed to be seen by the child, a screen is used to hide her. It is stood up near the crib at the beginning of the test period so that its introduction may not prove a disturbing factor during the presentation of the test.

S Test 1. *Response to adult's glance.* The adult approaches the child's crib, bends over the child and attempts to have her glance meet that of the child. She remains in this position from one to two minutes.

+ Gazes into the examiner's eyes.

B Test 2. *Holding the head erect*. The Ex. lifts the child from the horizontal to the vertical position, supporting the back and buttocks of the child with one hand, the head and the shoulders with the other. Then she carefully withdraws the support from the head, prepared to return the support immediately if the child can not hold his head up and lets it fall forward and backward.

+ The head is held erect for several seconds.

B Test 3. *Holding the head up in the prone position.* The child is placed in a horizontal position on his stomach, the head between the two arms which are bent at the elbows. In most cases, if the child is at all capable of doing so, he lifts the head without further efforts on the part of the Ex., so as to avoid the unpleasant contact of the face with the under-surface. If the reaction does not take place in this way, it can be called forth by the introduction of a loud sound towards which the child turns, or by presenting an object. The Ex. may drum upon the table or whistle or move an object before the eyes of the child.

+ The head is lifted up from the under-surface.

B Test 4. *Head movement of flight*. The Ex. goes through the movement of cleaning the child's nose with a piece of cotton or gauze.

+ Restlessly turning the head from one side to the other. Turning the head away.

M Test 5. *Fright at a loud sound*. The Ex., out of the child's sight, claps loudly with her hands for five seconds or rattles a loud rattler for the same time.

+ Blinking, distorting the corners of the mouth, wrinkling the forehead, shaking and restless movements of the body, crying, sounds of displeasure, weeping, clenching the fists (partial reaction suffices).

M Test 6. *Searching head movements during prolonged sound*. A rattle is shaken a foot and a half away from the child, outside his field of vision. The Ex. must be hidden from the child.

+ Turning the head. The glance usually remains staring straight ahead.

M Test 7. *Focusing on an object*. A shiny object (we used a wooden disc 3½ inches in diameter covered with tin foil), or the face of the Ex. is brought into the line of vision of the child about a foot away from his face.

+ Quietly looking at the object or staring.

M Test 8. *Reaction to changing tone of voice*. The Ex. hides herself from the child and speaks for thirty seconds in a normal tone of voice. Then she suddenly begins to growl for thirty seconds. In place of the deep growling a falsetto tone may be substituted.

+ Blinking, distorting the corners of the mouth, wrinkling the forehead, shaking and restless movements of the body, crying sounds of displeasure, weeping, clenching the fists (partial reaction suffices).

O Tests 9 and 10. *Cooing and experimenting movements*. These cannot be aroused by any specially introduced stimuli. One must wait for their spontaneous appearance while observing the child during the test period. Experimenting movements are in all cases to be observed by the examiner herself. They are slow, quiet movements which the child himself observes. One of their characteristics is the fact that one and the same movement is repeated by the child several times in exactly the same way. Those in charge of the child can be questioned as to the occurrence of cooing.

+ Occurrence of cooing sounds and experimenting movements.

EXPLANATION OF THE TEST SERIES FOR THE TWO MONTHS OLD CHILD

Test 1.—Tests the first social reaction—that is, the first specific reaction to another human being whose glance from this point on affects the child's behavior in a way different from all other stimuli.

Tests 2 and 3.—Test bodily control in respect to spinal column. These reactions depend upon health, nourishment, and opportunities for exercise. Failure may call attention to a deficiency in any one of these factors, the correction of which can then be attempted.

Test 4.—Shows how the child of this age tries to rid himself of a disagreeable stimulus by flight.

Test 5.—Tests the negative emotional reaction toward intense auditory stimuli.

Test 6.—Tests the first active interest of the child in auditory stimuli.

Test 7.—Tests passive reaction to an optical sensory stimulus.

Test 8.—Tests memory. The child, being familiar with normal voice, reacts emotionally, frightened by the strangeness of the sound of the changed voice.

The Tests for the First Year of Life

Tests 9 and 10.—Test 9 (cooing) is not yet to be considered as a social phenomenon, but as a mere sound-play; together with experimental movements it is to be regarded as furnishing preparatory materials for later development.

III—TEST SERIES FOR THE THREE MONTHS OLD CHILD

S Test 1. *Returning the glance with smiling or cooing.* The adult approaches the child's crib, bends over the child and attempts to have her glance meet that of the child. She remains in this position from one to two minutes.

+ Smiling or cooing at the Ex.

B Test 2. *Holding the head and shoulders erect in the prone position.* The child is placed in a horizontal position on his stomach, the head between the two arms which are bent at the elbows.

+ Raising the head and shoulders from the under-surface. The child supports himself on his forearms.

B Test 3. *Flight movement of the whole body in response to tactile stimulation.* The Ex. goes through the movement of cleaning the child's nose with a piece of cotton or gauze.

+ Turning the head and other parts of the body away. The arms and pelvis usually remain unmoved.

M Test 4. *Looking for the source of a sound.* A rattle is shaken a foot and a half away from the child, outside his field of vision. The Ex. must be hidden from the child.

+ During the time of the sound the eyes are directed searchingly to all sides.

M Test 5. *Following moving objects with the eyes.* A shiny object or the face of the observer is brought into the child's field of vision, as in II, 7. When the eyes of the child become focused on the object, this is moved slowly sidewards and then back to the other side again.

+ The eyes follow the moving object.

M Test 6. *Changed reaction upon repeating the presentation of an auditory stimulus.* The sound of a shrill whistle is used as stimulus. This is presented six times for fifteen seconds each, each representation separated by intervals of thirty seconds. (If no results are obtained with this stimulus the test may be repeated using a deep growling tone, as in II, 6. If the test is repeated, a period of ten minutes should have elapsed since the first presentation. This time can be used for giving other test items.)

+ The reaction to the first presentation of the stimulus is negative. With the repetition of the stimulus the negative quality of the reaction gradually lessens—the child becomes less restless, cries less lustily, reacts for a shorter length of time. The reactions to the last presentation are neutral.

M Test 7. *Reaction to the disappearance of the human face.* The Ex. disappears suddenly.

+ The child looks for several seconds after the human face or shows some sort of negative expression—such as crying, wrinkling the brow, screwing the mouth.

M Test 8. *Mask test.* The Ex. brings her face 1½ feet away from the child and stares at him quietly for thirty seconds. Then she places a mask (one not too intensely colored—we used a yellow-brown rabbit's head) before the face, and remains in the same position.

+ Frightening and negative reaction (II, 8) when the mask appears.

M Test 9. *Imitating facial movements.* The Ex. brings her face close to that of the child (8 inches distant). While the child is looking the Ex. purses her mouth and broadens it out again, repeating this movement as long as the child watches attentively.

+ Every attempt of the child to imitate the movements while the Ex. is demonstrating them or afterward. Often the child does not succeed in producing the same movements but similar ones. Demonstrating must often be continued from three to ten minutes.

O Test 10. *Feeling of objects* (*active touch*). A piece of cardboard (4 x 8 inches) is brought near the hands of the child, in such a way that the child comes in contact with it through one of his movements. Any other firm object can be substituted for the cardboard.

+ The child passes his flat hand or clenched fist over the cardboard several times. The movement is slow and observed by the child. This reaction can often be seen without the introduction of any particular stimulus if the child's hand accidentally comes in contact with the railing of the crib or the clothing of the Ex.

EXPLANATION OF THE TEST SERIES FOR THE THREE MONTHS OLD CHILD

Test 1.—Tests a social reaction in as much as smiling occurs at this age only as a reaction to people.

Test 2.—Tests bodily control in respect to spinal column. These reactions depend upon health, nourishment, and opportunity for exercise. Failure may call attention to a deficiency in any one of these factors, the correction of which can then be attempted.

Test 3.—Tests a more effective reaction than II, 4.

Test 4.—Tests the first eye-ear coördination. This is important as the eye from now on furnishes the child's main organ of orientation.

Test 5.—Tests the beginning of an active interest in optical sensory stimuli.

Tests 6, 7, and 8.—Test memory.

6.—With an auditory stimulus. Through familiarization with the stimulus the shock to the organism becomes less.

7.—In a social situation.

8.—Is comparative to II, 8, with the visual stimulus of the human face instead of the auditory stimulus of the human voice.

Test 9.—Tests imitation on a reflective level, hence no exact imitation can be expected.

Test 10.—Tests reaction to tactile qualities of an object, which is considered to be a preparatory stage for later manipulation of objects.

IV—TEST SERIES FOR THE FOUR MONTHS OLD CHILD

S Test 1. *Expression of displeasure when adult stops playing with the child.* The Ex. occupies herself with the child, plays with him, speaks to him or sings to him and then stops suddenly.

+ Expressions of displeasure.

B Test 2. *Lying supported only by the palms of the hands.* The child is placed in a horizontal position on his stomach, the head between the two arms which are bent at the elbows.

+ Head and shoulders, and the upper part of the body as well, are raised up from the under-surface, so that the child is supported only by his palms.

B Test 3. *Grasping with both hands without using the fingers.* A rattle is moved within reaching distance of the child. His attention is drawn to this.

+ Child reaches for rattle with both hands with fists clinched or spread out. Does not make use of ability to close the hand in grasping.

B Test 4. *Grasping a touched object.* An object out of sight is so placed that the child's hand comes in contact with it.

+ The touched object is grasped.

B Test 5. *Diaper experiment in lying position.* A nontransparent diaper of close weave is laid on the face of the child.

+ Restless tossing about of the body.

M Test 6. *Active looking about in a new situation.* The Ex. carries child into another part of the room.

+ Active looking about in the new situation.

M Test 7. *Positive reaction to light.* The child is

brought into a semi-dark room. A cloth is hung over the bed, or a screen placed between the crib and the source of light. A flash-light (3 volt) is then brought up to within 6 inches from the face of the child, into his line of vision, and is lighted. It is turned off when the child ceases to regard the light. If the child does not regard the light, it is turned off after ten seconds. After an interval of twenty seconds the procedure is repeated. The light stimulus is presented five times in this way. The Ex. must be hidden from the child behind a screen.

+ Either the reaction to the first presentation is positive and remains so throughout, or the first neutral perception is superseded by a positive reaction.

M Test 8. *Looking at an object while moving it.* A rattle is placed in the child's hand; hand holds it firmly, even if it is not yet engaged in active grasping.

+ Looks at the object in his hand.

M Test 9. *Imitating facial expressions.* The Ex. brings her face close to that of the child, as in III, 9. The demonstrated movement is wrinkling of the forehead. The Ex. brings horizontal and vertical lines to her brow. The movement must be repeated several times.

+ Every attempt to imitate the movements while the examiner is demonstrating them or afterward.

O Test 10. *Manipulatory movement of an object.* A rattle is placed in the child's hand; hand holds it firmly, even if it is not yet engaged in active grasping.

+ Child holds rattle firmly and moves it about.

The Tests for the First Year of Life

Test 1.—Tests the positive reaction toward attention of the other person and a negative reaction if the attention ceases.

Test 2.—Tests bodily control in respect to spinal column. These reactions depend upon health, nourishment, and opportunity for exercise. Failure may call attention to a deficiency in any one of these factors, the correction of which can then be attempted.

Tests 3 and 4.—Test early stages of grasping. Grasping is the best index for the activity of the child.

Test 5.—Tests flight movements in a more complicated situation.

Tests 6 and 7.—Test further development in active interest for visual stimuli.

Test 8.—Tests the first coördination of visual and tactile impressions.

Test 9.—Tests imitation on a reflective level, hence no exact imitation can be expected.

Test 10.—First manipulation of objects, which must be considered as a further development in the mastery of life.

V—TEST SERIES FOR THE FIVE MONTHS OLD CHILD

S Test 1. *Reflecting friendly and angry facial expressions.* Ex. bends over the child, brings her face close to his (10 inches away), smiles and addresses him in a friendly fashion for thirty seconds. Suddenly she changes her tone, wrinkles her brows, and talks to the child angrily.

+ Smiling and positive expressional movements in answer to the friendly attitude, negative expressional movements in answer to the angry attitude.

B Test 2. *Holding the head and shoulders high in the dorsal position.* A shiny object—a disc such as described before, or a mirror (6 x 8 inches)—is brought from the foot of the crib towards the child, to catch his eye, and then moved back again. If the child is momentarily preoccupied with some objects held in his hand, these can be taken away from him and moved toward the foot of the bed.

+ Head and shoulders are raised up from undersurface.

B Test 3. *Turning from back to side and back again.* A bell is rung in a position at the side of the child where it can be seen, or else it is brought in reach of the child in such a way that it can be attained by a slight turning sidewards. Desired reaction often occurs during the test period without special efforts on the part of the Ex.

+ Turning the whole body to the side. The item is passed when the pelvis is also turned.

B Test 4. *Grasping an object in view with one hand.* (As in IV, 3.)

+ The child grasps an object with one hand, clutching it with his fingers. The item is also passed if the child grasps it with both hands and uses his fingers in so doing.

B Test 5. *Diaper experiment in dorsal position.* A non-transparent diaper of close weave is laid on the face of the child.

+ The child grasps diaper and extricates himself from it.

M Test 6. *Positive reaction to sounds.* A bell is rung near the child. The Ex. is hidden from him.

+ Smiling and positive expressional movements.

M Test 7. *Reaction to the withdrawal of a toy.* A toy the child is manipulating is suddenly taken away.

+ Expressions of displeasure.

M Test 8. *Looking for a lost toy.* The child is observed when he accidentally loses a toy, or else a toy is taken out of his hands, without using any force.

+ Child turns his head in the direction in which the toy disappeared and looks about searchingly.

M Test 9. *Imitating facial expressions.* The Ex. bends over the child and shows him how she sticks her tongue in and out.

+ Every attempt of the child to imitate the movements while the Ex. is demonstrating them or afterward. Often the child does not succeed in producing the same movements but similar ones. Demonstrating must often be continued from three to ten minutes.

O Test 10. *Defense reaction to the withdrawal of a toy.* A toy which the child has been manipulating is suddenly taken out of his hands.

+ Some sort of resistance is shown to the Ex., who tries to take the toy out of the child's hand.

The First Year of Life

Test 1.—Tests the beginning of social differentiation. Before this the child reacts positively to all social approaches. At this stage the mood of the adult would seem to be transferred to the child and his facial expressions to result from this transferred mood.

Tests 2 and 3.—Test bodily control in respect to spinal column. These reactions depend upon health, nourishment, and opportunities for exercise. Failure may call attention to a deficiency in any one of these factors, the correction of which can then be attempted.

Test 4.—Tests further development in grasping.

Test 5.—The first adequate and specific reaction to a hindrance; the child not only rids himself of it, but does so in the quickest and most effective way.

Test 6.—The first positive emotions toward an auditory stimulus.

Test 7.—Shows the first desire to possess a toy through the negative emotional attitude to its withdrawal.

Test 8.—Further development of memory: memory of an object.

Test 9.—Tests imitation on a reflective level, hence no exact imitation can be expected.

Test 10.—Shows the first desire to possess a toy through the child's positive efforts to keep it.

The Tests for the First Year of Life

S Test 1. *Actively seeking contact.* The Ex. stands next to the crib without regarding the child in any way, and avoids looking at the child's face.

+ Attempts on the part of the child to set up a contact: cooing, looking.

S Test 2. *Distinguishing between friendly and angry talking.* The Ex. is hidden from the child. She talks to the child for thirty seconds in friendly tones and then for thirty seconds in angry tones.

+ Positive expressional movements in response to the friendly address, and negative expressional movements in response to the scolding address.

B Test 3. *Sitting with support.* The Ex. sets the child up in a sitting position in a corner of his crib and supports him with a cushion behind his back.

+ The child remains erectly seated.

B Test 4. *Diaper experiment in prone position.* The child is brought into a horizontal position, on his stomach (see II, 3). A diaper is laid over his head and the corners of the front part drawn back over the shoulders, so that the diaper closes in over the face.

+ The child extricates himself by grasping the diaper with his hands.

B Test 5. *Table-edge test.* The Ex. seats herself in front of a table and takes the child on her lap so that he can reach the table with outstretched arms.

+ The child grasps the table edge.

M Test 6. *Displeasure at unsuccessful grasping.* See IV, 3. As soon as the child reaches for the object, it is withdrawn.

+ Crying or other negative expressions.

M Test 7. *Smiling as a general reaction.* As a rule this type of smiling, not to be designated as social, occurs spontaneously at some time during the test period. The child smiles at his own movements or at some object he sees or in response to touch (tickling or stroking). The Ex. can try to evoke this reaction if it does not occur of itself.

+ Smiling in response to something other than the human face or voice.

M Test 8. *Expectation in response to the repetition of a stimulus.* A shiny metal bell is brought to the child's view and left there ten seconds, during which time the Ex. rings the bell softly. After an interval of ten seconds this is repeated; it is done again and again until the bell has been presented six times.

+ When the bell is no longer to be seen after the sixth presentation, the child directs his gaze, after prolonged searching, back to the aperture in the screen whence the bell appeared and was returned again. The interest is actively directed to the stimulus which has not reappeared. Generally a sound characteristic of expectancy is emitted.

M Test 9. *Imitating sounds.* The Ex. bends over the child and makes the sound of a drawn-out, guttural "re-re-re" several times.

+ Every attempt to make a sound which has any claim

to similarity with that made by the Ex. This may occur as an immediate or retarded response.

O Test 10. *Manipulation on a stationary object with a moving object.* The child is given a rattle or a stick to play with and is then brought near to another object leaning against the wall or the crib railing; or else an object is dangled close to him so that he can hit at it with the rattle.

+ The child holds one object in his hand and hits at a second object with it.

EXPLANATION OF THE TEST SERIES FOR THE SIX MONTHS OLD CHILD

Test 1.—Marks the turning point from the passive to the active social attitude.

Test 2.—Permits us to speak of the first social understanding, as the child, not seeing the adult, cannot reflect her expressions nor can he here be reacting to the sensory stimulus of the change in tone of the voice itself, as this is strictly avoided by the Ex.

Test 3.—Tests bodily control in respect to spinal column. These reactions depend upon health, nourishment, and opportunities for exercise. Failure may call attention to a deficiency in any one of these factors, the correction of which can then be attempted.

Test 4.—The situation of V, 5 is complicated by a postural difficulty.

Test 5.—Shows the predominating tendency of this age to grasp. The child will grasp at even so unlikely an object as the table-edge.

Test 6.—In testing, the negative reaction to a hindered attainment is the first proof that the child has set himself a goal.

Test 7.—Shows smiling for the first time as a positive expression in response to a situation no longer specifically social.

Test 8.—Is a further step in memory development. The child does not only miss the object that has been removed, but also bears in mind the whole situation of occurrence and recurrence.

Test 9.—Tests the first active imitation, since sounds cannot by their very nature be merely reflected.

Test 10.—Further manipulatory development. The first use of an object as a tool.

VII—TEST SERIES FOR THE SEVEN MONTHS OLD CHILD

S Test 1. *Distinguishes between angry and friendly facial expressions.* The Ex. bends over the child and looks at him for a while in a friendly way. Then she changes her expression, wrinkles her brow, and looks angrily at the child.

+ Positive reaction to the friendly and negative reaction to the angry face. This item is passed only when appropriate expressional movements other than those made by the Ex. are used.

B Test 2. *Locomotion.* This reaction cannot be evoked experimentally. It is, however, bound to appear during the half hour or so in which the Ex. is occupied with the child, if he is capable of performing it.

+ The child turns from his back on to his side, from

the side on to his stomach, on to the other side, and on to the back again. Or he may move sidewise in some other manner.

B Test 3. *Diaper experiment in the supported sitting position.* The child is in the position described in VI, 3, and the diaper is laid over his head as in VI, 4.

+ The child removes the diaper with his hands without toppling over in the process.

B́ Test 4. *Moving toward a desired object by changing the position.* A rattle (if this does not sufficiently rouse the child's interest, a rubber or cloth animal may be substituted) is brought close to the child so that he can see it, but cannot reach it without changing his position. One can place the toy near the child on his pillow or can hold it in the direction of his glance in such a way that he can attain it only by lifting his head and shoulders or by some other change of position.

+ The child makes some move toward the object in addition to reaching for it.

B Test 5. *Pushing away a stimulus.* The Ex. goes through the movement of cleaning the child's· nose with a piece of cotton or gauze.

+ The child grasps the Ex.'s hand and pushes it away from his face.

M Test 6. *Loss of interest in a repeated stimulus.* The child is brought into a semi-dark room. A cloth is hung over the bed, or a screen is placed between the crib and the source of light. A flash-light (3 volt) is then brought up to within 15 cm. of the face of the child, into his line of vision, and is lighted. It is turned off when the child ceases to regard the light. If the child does not regard the light, it is turned off after ten seconds. After an interval of twenty seconds the procedure is repeated. The light stimulus is presented five times in this way. The Ex. must be hidden from the child behind a screen for this test.

+ The child turns actively and attentively toward the light at its first presentation. With repetition the positive reaction turns into one of indifference. (Grasping or feeling of the flash-light is to be avoided.)

M Test 7. *Imitating knocking.* The Ex. knocks on the railing of the crib with a rattle and then hands the rattle to the child, who is lying close to the railing.

+ Every movement made by the child similar to those made by the adult.

O Test 8. *Taking a toy away from an adult.* The Ex. quietly places her hand, which holds a rattle, within reach of the child in his crib.

+ The child tries, with some show of strength, to take the toy away from the adult.

O Test 9. *The paper test.* A piece of white writing paper (15cm. x 20cm.) is put into the child's hand.

+ The child crushes, rolls, or tears the paper, or changes its form in some other way.

O Test 10. *Manipulating and moving two objects.* While the child is occupying himself with a rattle, another is offered him.

+ The child holds both objects and moves them about.

The Tests for the First Year of Life

Test 1.—Is not to be confused with V, 1. The reaction here is clearly one of understanding an optical situation corresponding to the auditory situation in VI, 2.

Test 2.—Tests bodily control in the first locomotion.

Test 3.—The situation of V, 5 is complicated by a postural difficulty.

Test 4.—Tests the first coördination between locomotion and grasping.

Test 5.—Further development of defense activity.

Test 6.—Illustrates a turning point in the development, in as much as heretofore the child has reacted with fright to strange stimuli (see II, 8), and now becomes bored with the familiar.

Test 7.—Tests imitation of a function involving the use of material.

Test 8.—The child's interest in an object is now so keen that he is no longer satisfied with the things that are given to him, but exerts himself to obtain that which he sees in some one else's possession.

Test 9.—Tests the first activity directed to changing the form of an object.

Test 10.—Further manipulatory development.

VIII—TEST SERIES FOR THE EIGHT MONTHS OLD CHILD

B Test 1. *Sitting alone.* The child is seated in the middle of the crib without any support.

+ The child remains erectly seated.

B Test 2. *Crawling.* This reaction occurs usually without introducing a special stimulus.

+ The child moves about—forward, or sidewise—crawling.

B Test 3. *Reaching for an object outside the crib.* A toy is placed outside the crib at the same level on which the child is lying, within his reach.

+ The child stretches out his arm through the crib railing and takes the toy.

M Test 4. *Neutral reaction to single stimulus.* The optical stimulus of IV, 7 or the auditory stimulus of VI, 8 is used.

+ The child reacts neutrally showing indifference to the stimulus. (Reaction to either optical or auditory stimulus suffices.)

M Test 5. *The mirror test.* A hand mirror (6 x 8 inches) is held up to the child about 10 inches away from him.

+ The child smiles at his reflection in the mirror and regards it with interest.

M Test 6. *Reaction to strange surroundings.* The child is brought into a strange room, or else his familiar surroundings are altered—for instance, his crib is altered by having a dark cloth hung over it with only a small opening left for purposes of observation.

+ Negative expressional movements—at least a weak negative astonishment.

M Test 7. *Imitating squeezing the doll.* The Ex. squeezes a rubber doll so as to make it squeak several times while the child is looking. She then holds it out to him.

+ Every attempt of the child to imitate the movements made by the adult.

M Test 8. *Persisting reaction to withdrawal of a toy.* A toy the child is manipulating is suddenly taken away.

+ The child shows signs of displeasure and remains in a negative mood for a period after the withdrawal.

M Test 9. *Deliberate choice of a toy.* The Ex. holds out two different toys (a rattle and a rubber animal), one in each hand within the reach of the child and waits until the child grasps one of them. She then takes this toy away from him and holds the two toys out again in the same way with their position in respect to right and left interchanged.

+ The child takes the same toy the second time as the first time.

O Test 10. *Preferring paper to other objects.* A child preoccupied with another object is presented with a piece of paper (see VII, 9). After he has been manipulating the paper the original toy is substituted for it, and then the child is offered the paper for the second time.

+ The child drops the toy immediately and devotes himself exclusively to the paper.

EXPLANATION OF THE TEST SERIES FOR THE EIGHT
MONTHS OLD CHILD

Test 1.—Tests bodily control in respect to spinal column. These reactions depend upon health, nourishment, and opportunities for exercise. Failure may call attention to a deficiency in. any one of these factors, the correction of which can then be. attempted.

Test 2:—Further development in locomotion.

Test 3.—Tests further coördination between. locomotion and grasping.

Test 4.—Shows that the child, who, during the first half year, was able to master only single stimuli, is now no longer interested in them, but is interested in the configuration and organization of stimuli.

Test 5.—Shows this interest in configuration exemplified by the reflection in the mirror.

Test 6.—Tests memory as in II, 8—this being a situation in place of a single stimulus.

Test 7.—Further development of imitation. See VII, 7.

Test 8.—Emotional reaction in connection with further development of the desire for an object.

Test 9.—Tests the beginning of will, showing the first conscious goal in the definite choice of one. object.

Test 10.—Shows that the child is interested in the process of changing the form of an object more than he is in mere functioning.

IX—TEST SERIES FOR THE NINE MONTHS OLD CHILD

S Test 1. *Becoming accustomed to a strange adult.*

+ The child who regarded the Ex. at first somewhat fearfully or cried changes his attitude during the test period. He smiles at the Ex. or is, at any rate, no longer moved to a negative response.

S Test 2. *Arousing an adult's attention.* The Ex. stands beside the child but turns her back to him and is apparently occupied with other things.

+ Attempts to direct the adult's attention to himself by pulling at her dress, offering her a toy, and directing vocalizations at her.

S Test 3. *Understanding gestures.* The Ex. comes up to the child, who is watching her, and shakes her finger at him threateningly for thirty seconds. After a short interval she stretches out her hands welcomingly and invites him towards her with movements. At the same time she endeavors to keep her face as expressionless and unchanging as possible.

+ A negative reaction, negative expressional movements, and drawing back in response to the threatening gesture; and positive reaction, expressional movements, smiling, and bending towards the Ex. in response to the inviting gestures.

S Test 4. *Playing cuckoo.* The Ex. covers the child's face with a diaper. After ten seconds she lifts this up, after ten seconds places it over the child's face again, etc. When she places it she says, "Cuckoo," and when she lifts it up, "Da da."

+ The child glances with interest in the direction from which the Ex.'s face appears and greets her appearance with smiling.

B Test 5. *Kneeling with support.* The Ex. sets the child in a kneeling position, supporting him at the back and chest.

+ The child holds this position.

B Test 6. *Grasping two objects while sitting alone.* The child is sitting by himself and is given first one and then a second toy (rattle and rubber doll).

+ The child grasps the second object without letting go of the first or toppling from his sitting position.

M Test 7. *Curiosity for that which is hidden.* A piece of stiff paper is rattled, or a metronome is set ticking behind the screen.

+ The child searches for the source of the sound, tries to look around the screen or through the aperture. Expressions of attention, interest, and curiosity.

M Test 8. *Imitating opening and shutting the picture book.* The Ex. opens and shuts a picture book (8 x 4½ inches) several times while the child is watching her. She then gives him the book.

+ Every attempt to imitate the adult's handling of the book.

MO Test 9. *The pocket test.* While the child is watching her the Ex. puts a toy in the pocket of her apron which is close enough so that the child can reach it with a small movement.

+ The child takes the object out of the pocket.

O Test 10. *"Destructive" activity.* For this item a nest of six hollow blocks is used; ours ranged in size from 4 to 1½ inches. The Ex. uses these to build a tower for the child.

+ The child tries to knock the tower down.

The Tests for the First Year of Life

Test 1.—Shows the first differentiation between strange and familiar persons, in as much as it is necessary to become accustomed to the adult before positive reactions occur.

Test 2.—Further development of active contact seeking.

Test 3.—Tests the understanding of gestures as distinguished from the imitation. This is guaranteed by the fact that the child responds not with gestures but with the appropriate reaction called for by the gestures.

Test 4.—Shows (1) that the mastery of the situation is so complete that it becomes a form of play for the child, and shows (2) the first organized play, characterized by a rhythmical sequence of a behavior pattern.

Test 5.—Tests bodily control in respect to spinal column. These reactions depend upon health, nourishment, and opportunities for bodily exercise. Failure may call attention to a deficiency in any one of these factors, the correction of which can then be attempted.

Test 6.—Further development in postural control and grasping. The performances which were heretofore accomplished singly are now accomplished together at the same time.

Test 7.—The beginnings of curiosity, which may be evidence of the first imagery.

Test 8.—Tests imitation of a function involving the use of material.

Test 9.—Further development of memory, combined with activity directed towards an object.

Test 10.—This activity is not destructive from the child's point of view, since the child does not perceive the tower of blocks as a product of the building. He sees only the functioning of the building process itself.

X—TEST SERIES FOR THE TEN MONTHS OLD CHILD

S Test 1. *Turning in astonishment to an adult.* The Ex. makes a sudden sound with a shrill whistle or flashes a light into the child's eyes.

+ The child looks questioningly at the Ex.

S Test 2. *Organized play with an adult.* The Ex. gives the child a toy and takes it away again, gives it back and takes it away again, etc. Each time when she takes it away, she says, "Thank you."

+ The child enters into the game by giving and taking the object of his own accord.

B Test 3. *Standing with support.* The Ex. stands the child up so that he can grasp hold of the railing of the crib or some other support.

+ The child remains standing with this support.

B Test 4. *The diaper experiment while sitting alone.* While the child is sitting alone the diaper is placed over his head as in VI, 4.

+ The child removes the diaper without falling down.

B Test 5. *Throwing objects.* This item is not expressly evoked, but usually occurs spontaneously.

+ The child does not merely drop an object, but actually throws it, lifting it up first.

M Test 6. *The glass plate test.* A plate of glass 19½ inches long and 11¾ inches wide is placed in front of the child, and a toy, to which the child's attention has been called, is placed behind the glass.

+ The child reaches around behind the glass plate, and grasps the toy.

M Test 7. *Imitating ringing the bell.* The Ex. swings the bell to make it ring and hands it to the child.

+ Every attempt to make the movements just demonstrated.

M Test 8. *Memory test.* A box containing a ball is given to the child for five minutes. The box is then taken away and returned after thirty seconds without the ball.

+ The child looks for the ball, and turns in astonishment to the Ex.

MO Test 9. *Uncovering a covered object.* While the child is watching, the Ex. covers a toy with a cloth.

+ The child takes the cover off the toy and then takes the toy.

O Test 10. *Opening a box.* A cardboard box (6 x 4 x 2½ inches) with a loosely fitting cover is given to the child, closed.

+ The child opens the box.

EXPLANATIONS OF THE TEST SERIES FOR THE TEN
MONTHS OLD CHILD

Test 1.—Shows that the child conceives the adult as an effective being and sees in her the cause of the astonishing phenomenon.

Test 2.—Shows (1) that the mastery of the situation is so complete that it becomes a form of play for the child, and shows (2) organized play, characterized by a rhythmical sequence of a behavior pattern.

Test 3.—Tests bodily control in respect to spinal column. These reactions depend upon health, nourishment, and opportunities for exercise. Failure may call attention to a deficiency in any one of these factors, the correction of which can then be attempted.

Test 4.—The situation of V, 5 is complicated by a postural difficulty.

Test 5.—Tests a striking characteristic of this age.

Test 6.—Tests the first understanding of relations, as the child must perceive that the object lies behind the transparent wall and can be reached only by circumventing the glass.

Test 7.—Tests imitation of a function involving the use of material.

Test 8.—Further memory development—recall.

Test 9.—Further development of memory, combined with activity directed toward an object.

Test 10.—Manipulatory development.

The Tests for the First Year of Life

S Test 1. *Organized play with an adult.* The child lies on his back and the Ex. places a diaper over his face and takes it away as in IX, 4.

+ After several repetitions the child places the diaper over his face and takes it away himself.

B Test 2. *Rising to the sitting position.* A toy is held out to the child in such a way that he cannot reach it from the lying position.

+ The child raises himself to the sitting position.

M Test 3. *Memory test.* The empty box, as used in X, 8, is presented after an interval of ten minutes.

+ The child misses the contents of the box.

M Test 4. *Imitating beating two spoons together.* The Ex. beats two spoons together while the child is watching and then gives him the spoons.

+ Attempts to imitate this movement.

M Test 5. *Imitating sounds.* The Ex. pronounces very slowly and distinctly certain syllables: mamma, papa, dada, lala, etc.

+ Attempts to produce similar sounds.

M Test 6. *Fear of the unfamiliar.* Anything which is new to the child can be used for this item—a new toy, a strange person, or a strange situation.

+ Negative reaction.

M Test 7. *Pulling an object by its string.* A rattle or

bell with a string attached is placed out of the child's reach. The end of the string is placed near or in the child's hand.

+ The child pulls the toy toward him by means of the string.

O Test 8. *Careful handling of a block.* The six blocks are taken apart (the nest of blocks described in IX, 10) and placed before the child.

+ In his activity with the blocks the child sets a block down with all the signs of attention and care.

O Test 9. *Fitting hollow blocks into one another.* See XI, 8.

+ The child puts the blocks together again, fitting the smaller ones into the larger.

O Test 10. *Opening a box.* This time the cover of the box (see X, 10) is tightly fitted on.

+ The child opens the box.

EXPLANATION OF THE TEST SERIES FOR THE ELEVEN
MONTHS OLD CHILD

Test 1.—Shows (1) that the mastery of the situation is so complete that it becomes a form of play for the child, and shows (2) organized play, characterized by a rhythmical sequence of a behavior pattern.

Test 2.—Tests bodily control in respect to spinal column. These reactions depend upon health, nourishment, and opportunities for exercise. Failure may call attention to a deficiency in any one of these factors, the correction of which can then be attempted.

The Tests for the First Year of Life

Test 3.—Further memory development: recall.

Test 4.—Tests imitation of a function involving the use of material.

Test 5.—Tests further active imitation, since sounds cannot by their very nature be merely reflected.

Test 6.—*Tests the first fear reaction.* Fear differs from fright in so far as it does not deal with present situations but with an anticipated situation on the basis of a disagreeable happening in the past. It therefore involves memory as well as imagery.

Test 7.—Tests a further step in the understanding of relations. The child now understands that the string is a means of obtaining the toy which is otherwise out of reach.

Test 8.—Is the beginning of the constructive use of materials.

Test 9.—Marks the discovery of the specific use of hollow blocks.

Test 10.—Is a further development in dexterity in the manipulation of materials.

CHAPTER IV

The Tests for the Second Year of Life

Series I—Tests 1 ; 0—1 ; 2 (+ 29)

S   1. Organized play: getting up and lying down.

B   2. Holding something while standing with support.

B   3. Holding something while walking with support.

M   4. Observing his image in the mirror.

M   5. Grasping at the reflection of a cracker in the mirror.

M   6. Searching for the vanished contents of a box.

M   7. Recalling the chicken.

M   8. Imitating squeezing the ball to make the chicken come out.

O   9. Rubbing or knocking two sticks together.

O   10. Taking a nest of blocks apart and putting them together again.

Series II—Tests 1 ; 3—1 ; 5 (+ 29)

S   1. Organized play with a ball.

S   2. Understanding a demand.

B   3. Walking alone.

B   4. Picking something up while standing alone.

M   5. Looking at a colored "picture."

M   6. Turning to an adult in astonishment at mirror-image.

M   7 and 8. Recalling the chicken and the contents of the box.

M   9. Imitating drumming with two sticks.

O   10. Putting blocks back into the box.

Series III—Tests 1 ; 6—1 ; 8 (+ 29)

S   1. Understanding a forbidding.

B   2. Holding something while walking alone.
B   3. Climbing.
M   4. Searching for the reflection behind the mirror.
M   5. Finding and taking a cracker from under one of two boxes.
M   6 and 7. Recalling the chicken and the contents of the box.
M   8. Startling at sight of the spinning top.
M   9. Reaching an object by means of a stick.
O   10. Respecting the work of another.

Series IV—Tests 1; 9—1; 11 ($+$ 29)

S   1. Interested observance of the mask.
S   2. Understanding a command.
B   3. Climbing up onto a chair.
M   4. Recognizing a picture.
M   5. Putting a watch to his ear upon command.
M   6 and 7. Recalling the chicken and the contents of the box.
M   8. Imitating grinding the music-box.
O   9. Fitting two hollow sticks into one another.
O   10. Placing blocks on top of one another.

TEST SERIES 2-1 FOR THE CHILD FROM 1; 0—1; 2 ($+$ 29)

S Test 1. *Organized play: getting up and lying down.* The Ex. seats the child on the bed. She holds his hands, pushes him gently into the dorsal position, then lifts .him into a sitting position again, repeating this play three or four times. She accompanies the movements with the words "up" and "down," or similar ones.

$+$ The child laughs while the Ex. is playing with him and enters into the game; i.e., he follows the Ex.'s movements willingly, or reaches of his own accord for her hands in order to raise himself to the sitting position again.

B Test 2. *Holding something while standing with support.* The child is placed in a standing position so that he can grasp the crib-railing or the Ex. with one hand. In the other hand the child should hold some toy (a ball, block, doll, or some other toy).

+ The child stands erect and holds an object at the same time.

B Test 3. *Holding something while walking with support.* The child is holding something as in Test 2 when the Ex. calls him to her.

+ The child walks with support and holds an object at the same time.

M Test 4. *Observing his image in the mirror.* The Ex. places a mirror in the child's hands so that he can see himself in it.

+ The child looks in the mirror and touches and feels of his image in it.

M Test 5. *Grasping at the reflection of a cracker in the mirror.* The mirror is placed about 6 inches away from the child's face. The Ex. holds a cracker next to the child's head in such a way that its reflection can be seen by him in the mirror. Touching the child's head with the hand or the cracker should be avoided, as this would furnish a clew to its position.

+ The child grasps at the mirror in his attempt to obtain the cracker. One reaction of this sort suffices, as it has been found that many children relinquish their purpose after one unsuccessful trial and then content themselves with merely looking at the mirror.

M Test 6. *Searching for the vanished contents of a box.* The Ex. sets down before the seated child a hollow block (the largest in the nest), open side down, and lets it stay this way for thirty seconds; if the child lifts the block, she takes it out of his hands and places it in the former position again. At the conclusion of the thirty seconds, the block is turned about so that the opening is on top, which manipulation may be left to the child. The Ex. then places the two little wooden eggs in the block so that the child can observe the procedure. She should occupy herself as much as possible with the block and its contents—take out and replace the eggs, shake the block so that it rattles—for a period of one minute. Block and contents are then removed, and the child's attention directed to something else during the three minutes which constitute the latent period for recognition at this age. At the conclusion of this interval, the block is again set before the child, open side down.

+ The child takes hold of the block immediately, turns it up and looks into it or shakes it. He shows astonishment over the fact that the expected contents are not to be found in it.

M Test 7. *Recalling the chicken.* The child is given the ball with the chicken and is shown how the chicken comes out when the ball is squeezed, and how it snaps back when the pressure on the ball is let go. The presentation lasts one minute. The Ex. then occupies the child's attention with something else for three minutes, this being the latent memory period for this age-level.

At the conclusion of this time, the child is given the ball without the chicken.[1]

+ The child shows distinct astonishment at the absence of the chicken. He squeezes the ball and looks questioningly at the Ex., or else examines the hole in the ball with his fingers.

Note.—This test must be given before Test 8.

M Test 8. *Imitating squeezing the ball to make the chicken come out.* The Ex. shows the child the ball with the chicken for one minute. She squeezes it and guides the child's hand in doing the same.

+ The child learns to squeeze the ball.

O Test 9. *Rubbing or knocking two sticks together.* The child is given two hollow sticks. His behavior with them is observed for five minutes.

+ The child rubs or knocks the two sticks one against the other.

O Test 10. *Taking a nest of blocks apart and putting them together again.* A nest of six hollow blocks is presented to the child. While he is looking, the Ex. takes them apart and sets them down in front of him. Once his interest in the blocks has been roused, his behavior with them is observed for five minutes. The Ex. should not show the child how the blocks are put together.

+ The child puts one block into another and takes it

[1] It sometimes happens that the child is afraid of the chicken. This does not interfere with the memory test, however, in as much as one can infer from expressions of displeasure occurring at the end of the latent period whether the child recognizes the ball or not.

out again at least once during the period of five minutes.

EXPLANATION OF TEST SERIES 2-I

Test 1.—Shows (1) that the mastery of the situation is so complete that it becomes a form of play for the child, and shows (2) organized play, characterized by a rhythmical sequence of a behavior pattern.

Tests 2 and 3.—Further development in postural control (see IX, 6).

Test 4.—The child is here not only interested in regarding his image as such, as in VIII, 5, but in the relationship of this reflection to other things. He shows this by his manipulative attempts.

Test 5.—Gives evidence that the relation between the reflection and the object has not as yet been fully grasped.

Tests 6 and 7.—Further tests of memory development.

Test 8.—Tests learning ability through imitation in connection with materials.

Test 9.—The first manipulation of two objects, directed against one another.

Test 10.—Further development of the specific use of hollow blocks.

TEST SERIES 2-II FOR THE CHILD FROM 1 ; 3—1 ; 5 (+ 29)

S Test 1. *Organized play with a ball.* The Ex. seats the child in a corner of his crib or on the floor and rolls the ball to him.

+ The child rolls the ball back to the Ex., repeating the play several times.

S Test 2. *Understanding a demand.* The Ex. demands a toy of the child with an appropriate gesture of the hand and the slowly, distinctly spoken words, "Give me that."

+ The child hands the toy to the Ex.

B Test 3. *Walking alone.* When the child is standing, the Ex. calls to him showing him a toy or a cracker.

+ The child walks to the Ex. without holding on to anything for support.

B Test 4. *Picking something up while standing alone.* When the child is standing, an object is placed at his feet. If he does not pick it up spontaneously, the Ex. can get him to do so by saying, "Give me that."

+ The child picks up the object without falling down and without holding on to a support.

M Test 5. *Looking at a colored "picture."* The child is given a color-card. After one minute—or sooner, if the child has lost interest in it—this is taken away and replaced by a figure-card. The color-card is a piece of cardboard 16 x 23 cm. covered with shiny red paper. The figure-card is the same with various figures cut out of colored paper pasted on it.

+ The child shows decidedly more interest for the figure-card and occupies himself with it more intensively. He manipulates the color-card, whereas he looks at the figure-card attentively, follows the contours of the figures with his fingers, etc.

The Tests for the Second Year of Life

M Test 6. *Turning to an adult in astonishment at mirror-image*. The child is given a mirror to hold.

+ The child observes his image in the mirror, looks about searchingly and up at the Ex. in a questioning manner.

M Tests 7 and 8. *Recalling the chicken and the contents of the box after eight minutes*. The Ex. sets down before the seated child a hollow block (the largest in the nest), open side down, and lets it stay this way for thirty seconds; if the child lifts the block, she takes it out of his hands and places it in the former position again. At the conclusion of the thirty seconds, the block is turned about so that the opening is on the top, which manipulation may be left to the child. The Ex. then places the two little wooden eggs in the block so that the child can observe the procedure. She should occupy herself as much as possible with the block and its contents—take out and replace the eggs, shake the block so that it rattles—for a period of one minute. Block and contents are then removed, and the child's attention is directed to something else during the three minutes which constitute the latent period for recognition at this age. At the conclusion of this interval, the block is again set before the child, open side down.

+ The child takes hold of the block immediately, turns it up and looks into it or shakes it. He shows astonishment over the fact that the expected contents are not to be found in it.

The child is given the ball with the chicken and is shown how the chicken comes out when the ball is squeezed, and how it snaps back when the pressure on the ball is let go. The presentation lasts one minute.

247

The Ex. then occupies the child's attention with something else for three minutes, this being the latent memory period for this age-level. At the conclusion of this time the child is given the ball without the chicken.

+ The child shows distinct astonishment at the absence of the chicken. He squeezes the ball and looks questioningly at the Ex., or else examines the hole in the ball with his fingers.

M Test 9. *Imitating drumming with two sticks.* The Ex. places a drum with two drumsticks within reach of the child and waits a minute to see whether he will begin to drum of his own accord. If this is not the case, as most often happens, the Ex. shows him how to drum and then turns the sticks over to him.

+ The child beats the drum with both sticks.

O Test 10. *Putting blocks back into the box.* The child is given a box with six blocks in it.

+ The child takes the blocks carefully out of the box and puts them back again. It suffices if four out of the six blocks are replaced.

EXPLANATION OF TEST SERIES 2-11

Test 1.—The child's mastery of himself and materials is now advanced to the point where he can combine manipulation of an object with the social give and take of an organized play procedure.

Test 2.—Child understands words and meaningful gestures; his reaction is a specific effect of the other person.

The Tests for the Second Year of Life

Test 3.—Further development in bodily control.

Test 4.—Further development in postural control and grasping. The performances which were heretofore accomplished singly are now accomplished together at the same time.

Test 5.—Shows the child's interest in forms and figures, in *Gestalten,* which is akin to the interests in relations common to this age period.

Test 6.—The mirror-image is here regarded by the child as a sort of mystery; he wants to know about it, and turns to the adult in seeking an explanation.

Tests 7 and 8.—Further memory development. (See 2-I, 6 and 7.)

Test 9.—Further imitative development.

Test 10.—Further specific use of hollow blocks.

TEST SERIES 2-III FOR THE CHILD FROM 1 ; 6—1 ; 8 (+ 29)

S Test 1. *Understanding a forbidding.* The child is given several toys to play with and the Ex. joins him in this for five or ten minutes. She then calls his attention to another toy by obvious manipulations with it. When the child reaches for this toy, she withdraws it and says, "You can't do that. Don't touch it." She repeats this as long as the child continues to reach for the toy.

+ The child understands the forbidding and shows this in some way.

B Test 2. *Holding something while walking alone.*

While in a standing position the child is given something to hold in his hand. The Ex. at some distance away then calls him to come to her.

+ The child walks without support and without dropping the object.

B Test 3. *Climbing.* A little stool or wooden box—or any object on which the child might easily step—is placed in front of the crib. The Ex. then holds a toy or cracker at a height such that the child cannot reach it with outstretched arms without climbing up on the improvised step.

+ The child climbs up onto the low object placed before him while holding on the railing of the crib for support.

M Test 4. *Searching for the reflection behind the mirror.* The mirror is placed about 6 inches away from the child's face.

+ The child looks at his reflection in the mirror for a while. He then turns the mirror around, examines the back of it, and looks for the reflection there.

M Test 5. *Finding and taking a cracker from under one of two boxes.* Two small boxes without covers, one red and one blue, are used for this test. They are placed upside down in front of the seated child. The Ex., having engaged the child's attention, places a cracker under one of the boxes. She then changes the position of the boxes and their contents with respect to left and right. The boxes should be sufficiently far apart to exclude the possibility of the child's picking up both at once.

+ The child reaches for the correct box and takes the cracker from under it. In order to avoid a chance success, three trials should be passed. In repeating the procedure, the cracker is not always placed under the same box.

M Tests 6 and 7. *Recalling the chicken and the contents of the box after eleven minutes.* (See 2-I, 6 and 7.)

M Test 8. *Startling at sight of the spinning top.* The Ex. spins a top before the child.

+ The child observes the spinning top in astonishment.

M Test 9. *Reaching an object by means of a stick.* At first the Ex. places a drumstick in the crib and allows the child to busy himself with it. A chair is set next to the crib just far enough away to avoid the child's reaching it with outstretched arms. The Ex. spins a top on the chair.

+ The child attempts to reach the top with outstretched arms and then tries to move it towards him with the use of the drumstick.

O Test 10. *Respecting the work of another.* The Ex. builds a tower out of the hollow blocks for the child.

+ The child observes the finished product attentively.

EXPLANATION OF TEST SERIES 2-III

Test 1.—Further understanding of words.

Test 2.—Further development, as in IX, 6.

Test 3.—Further development in bodily control.

Test 4.—Further investigatory activity in a search for understanding the relationships involved.

Test 5.—Tests memory and orientation. The child does not lose his orientation in following the movements and observing what is happening.

Tests 6 and 7.—Further tests of memory development.

Test 8.—The astonishment elicited here may be connected with the interest in relationships already referred to.

Test 9.—Thinking and acting in terms of a tool. See XI, 7.

Test 10.—The respect for another person's work forms the basis of the child's own constructions.

TEST SERIES 2-IV FOR THE CHILD FROM
1 ; 9—1 ; 11 (+ 29)

S Test 1. *Interested observance of the mask.* The Ex. first shows herself to the child as she is and then holds the mask in front of her face. In doing this she keeps her face close enough to the child for him to be able to reach it.

+ Every expression of interest or pleasure—e.g., the child stares attentively at the mask, he feels of it with his fingers, he tries to take it, he smiles at it.

S Test 2. *Understanding a command.* To the child who is either sitting or standing in his crib the Ex. says slowly and distinctly, "Lie down," or "Sit down." When the child has complied with this, she says, "Stand up."

+ The child sits down or lies down and stands up in response to a command.

B Test 3. *Climbing up onto a chair.* The child is placed in a standing position in front of a chair. The Ex. holds a cracker over the back of the chair.

+ The child climbs onto the chair and stands on it.

M Test 4. *Recognizing a picture.* The child is given a "nonsense picture" which it usually observes from all sides only to wave it about or lay it down. After a minute or so the Ex. gives him the picture of a nurse.

+ The child recognizes the picture: he points at the picture or at the face of the nurse and smiles at the Ex. If he can talk he may call the picture "Mamma," "Dolly," "Nurse," or something similar. When the Ex. asks, "Show me Mamma," the child may point at the nurse. One of these responses suffices for passing the test.

M Test 5. *Putting a watch to his ear upon command.* The Ex. holds a watch up to the child's ear and says slowly, "Tic-toc, tic-toc." She holds it up to her own ear and then gives it to the child, asking, "Where is the tic-toc?" Pointing to her own ear she says, "Show me the tic-toc."

+ In response to the question the child holds the watch to his ear, and in response to the demand holds it up to the Ex.'s ear.

M Tests 6 and 7. *Recalling the chicken and the contents of the box after seventeen minutes.* (See 2-I, 6 and 7.)

M Test 8. *Imitating grinding the music-box.* The Ex.

gives the child the music-box and waits for one minute to see whether he will turn the handle of his own accord. If he does not—as is usually the case—she shows him how this is done.

+ The child turns the handle at least once around. The direction of the turning is of no consequence for the test.

O Test 9. *Fitting two hollow sticks into one another.* See instructions for 2-I, 9.

+ The child fits the sticks into one another or attempts to do this.

O Test 10. *Placing blocks on top of one another.* The Ex. gives the child the hollow blocks as in 2-I, 10.

+ The child places at least two blocks on top of one another during a period of five minutes.

EXPLANATION OF TEST SERIES 2-IV

Test 1.—The element of the unfamiliar now arouses interest rather than fear or fright.

Test 2.—Child understands words and meaningful gestures; his reaction is a specific effect of another person.

Test 3.—Further postural development.

Test 4.—Recognition of an object in its two-dimensional representation.

Test 5.—Involves social reactions, imitative ability, and verbal understanding.

Tests 6 and 7.—Further tests of memory development.

Test 8.—Tests learning ability through imitation in connection with materials.

The Tests for the Second Year of Life

Test 9.—Further development in the understanding of relations in the realm of concrete materials.

Test 10.—Further development in the constructive manipulation of materials.

CHAPTER V

The Practical Reliability of the Tests

IN order to determine what developmental differences are due to environmental causes, we tested ten children in each month selected from a favorable milieu for purposes of comparison. It is self-evident that this less extensive material cannot be considered equally with that obtained from the nonfavored [1] children. It was impossible to test an equally large number of children from better environments because procuring children from private families met with great difficulties, in spite of the kindest coöperation on the part of some parents. The fact that the milieu of these children was not so homogeneous as that of the nonfavored explains certain minor irregularities in the results. An example of this is the developmental increment for the fourth month which, in comparison with that obtained for the nonfavored children, appears unduly large, and the developmental increment for the fifth month, which appears too small. In as much as we wish to make no use of this material for its own sake but only for purposes of comparison, no great importance need be attached to these irregularities. It is recognized, in general, that the development of favored children is more irregular than that of nonfavored.

[1] For want of a better terminology, the translator has used the words "favored" and "nonfavored" children as referring to children from more and less favorable environments respectively. The German terms used in the original are *gepflegt* and *ungepflegt*.

The Practical Reliability of the Tests

In a comparison of the test results of the two groups the following general facts were brought out. In the first four months no appreciable differences were found. The favored children are not yet superior in development to the nonfavored children of the same age. Their first advance is found in the fifth month. From this point on the deviation increases with age until it amounts to one month at the end of the first year. The question now is: Along which lines do these differences manifest themselves?

On the basis of the experience which we have had with these test series within the last two years we wish to make a statement as to their practical reliability. In particular there are three questions which we shall consider:

1. In what cases is there a practical necessity for testing such young children?

2. What educational measures can be deduced from the test results?

3. In how far does the prognosis which is made on the basis of the test results agree with the actual course of the child's further development?

1. Psychological Judgments of Forty-five Children—Reasons for Subjecting Children to Tests

Questions one and two above will be answered on the basis of forty-five psychological judgments which we made during the course of several months in the Children's Clearing House in Vienna in connection with the tests for the first and second year.[2] Among the forty-

[2] For their assistance in the testing I am indebted to Dr. L. Danziger, E. Herzfeld, and L. Koller; for the re-testing, to the Misses Gindl and Jaenschke.

five children examined there were six retarded children who were more than 1; 11, but for whom the test-series of the second year sufficed. Twenty children were designated as retarded on the basis of the examination results. In the case of fourteen children developmental acceleration was found, and in the case of eleven children the developmental age was representative of the chronological age. From these figures we see already that the majority of children who come up for testing deviate from the average in some way, and, as a matter of fact, an examination is deemed necessary by the doctor, the nurse, or the parents because something in the child strikes them as different from the usual in children of his age. It is the task of the psychologist to analyze this difference further. There are also cases, of course, where a child comes up for testing without having any unusual feature. He may, for example, have been in unfavorable circumstances during a longer period of time (poverty or institutional life) or he may have a feeble-minded mother or a father who is a drinker or a syphilitic, and it is feared that the child may in some way be abnormal. Finally, there are also a few parents who, even as they might take a healthy child to the physician in order that he discover an unnoticed ailment which can be checked before any harm is worked, take their child to the psychologist for an examination as a matter of precaution. In 85 per cent of all the cases in which we tested children, the question was one of some striking deviation. To be sure, in general the children were designated by a physician or a nurse as striking—in other words, by individuals who were experienced in the observation of children and differ in this respect markedly from the average parent.

The Practical Reliability of the Tests

In this connection we must distinguish two groups of children: *Children who are striking only in some physical respect, and children who deviate from the average in their general developmental attainment or some general peculiarity.*

A. CHILDREN WITH STRIKING PHYSICAL DEVIATIONS

Among the children who deviate in physical respects there are:

1. Those who are physically very well, or very poorly, developed.

2. Sick children (curvature of the spine, eye diseases, inherited syphilis, glandular disturbances).

3. Children with abnormalities (microcephaly). Children whose physical condition was influenced by temporary ailments are not included under these three heads.

In all cases of *children within the first year of life who were designated by the physician as physically well-developed, the developmental age agreed with the chronological age,* and in many a decided developmental advance was observed.

We submit several examples:[3]

	C.A.	D.A.
B 548 *	0 ; 6	0 ; 6
B 675	0 ; 9	0 ; 10
B 768	0 ; 6	0 ; 7
B 870	0 ; 4	0 ; 5

* The children are designated by their protocol numbers.

In the second year a good physical development appears no longer to go unconditionally hand in hand

[3] In practical work it suffices in general to express the age of the child in the number of completed months, not reckoning with the exact number of days.

with good general development. As a matter of fact, good physical development can hide from the superficial observer poor mental ability. Instructive in this connection is the case of B 686, C.A. 1 ; 0, to whom we shall refer again later. His developmental age was found to be 1 ; 1, an acceleration of one month. This result, when compared with the general impression which he made, was startling. Closer analysis of the test result showed that B 686 passed easily all tests of bodily control up to the twenty-first month, but in the case of almost all tests in which some sort of perception of relations was demanded, as in pulling an object by its string, placing hollow blocks one within the other, the test with the stick, with the plate of glass, the pocket test, etc., he failed completely.

This is his protocol :

B 686 C.A.—1 ; 0 D.A.—1 ; 1					
	0 ; 9	0 ; 10	0 ; 11	1 ; 0	1 ; 3	1 ; 6
1	+	+	—	—	—	—
2	+	+	+	+	+	+
3	+	+	—	+	—	+
4	+	+	+	—	+	—
5	+	+	+	—	—	—
6	+	—	+	—	—	—
7	+	+	—	—	—	—
8	+	+	+	—	—	—
9	—	—	—	—	—	—
10	+	—	—	—	—	—

In general, the reverse is true of children whose physical condition is designated as poor. Even the abilities in such cases where pure bodily control is not demanded are influenced to a great extent. G 515, C.A., 1 ; 0, who was physically developed to the level of a six months old child (her weight was 13.4 pounds), had a physical retardation which was decidedly greater than her general retardation. The result of the test showed her D.A. to be 0; 8. Already at the seven-months level she failed those test items in which bodily control was of significance—namely: locomotion, manipulation of two objects, and knocking. The items which were passed at the eight- and nine-months levels are all independent of the factor of body control.

G 515 C.A.—1 ; 0 D.A.—0 ; 8				
0 ; 5	0 ; 6	0 ; 7	0 ; 8	0 ; 9
+	+	+	—	+
+	—	—	—	+
+	+	+	+	—
+	—	+	—	—
+	+	+	+	—
+	+	+	—	—
+	+	—	—	—
+	+	+	+	—
+	+	+	—	+
+	+	—	—	+

To be sure, the extent of the physical retardation is not always the same as the retardation along other lines. For example: B 646, C.A., 1; 1, who had curvature of the spine, was unable to perform the body control tests of the seventh and eighth months; his ability to handle materials was also limited, although grasping was well-developed; sense perception and memory, social behavior and imitative ability, however, corresponded very nearly to his chronological age.

We found no child who showed developmental acceleration in the face of physical retardation or illness. It must be left to later investigations to throw light upon the influence of single illnesses upon the course of development; likewise, upon the significance of various abnormalities, such as peculiar shape of the skull. A child with a sugar-loaf skull—B 672, C.A., 0; 4, for example—was accelerated by one month in his development; the microcephalic girl, G 709, C.A., o; 4, had a developmental age of two months. We are able, however—and this is most important practically—to show by means of careful analysis of the test results the difference existing between physical condition and general developmental level. We see that *no child can be termed gifted or not gifted solely on the basis of good or poor physical development*. Physically poorly developed children who have generally good abilities may still receive a good prognosis as long as there is a possibility of helping the physical condition. An example of this is the case of G 515, who was helped by intensive care. In cases similar to this a physician must be called upon. Where physical disability goes hand in hand with general inability of performance, in addition to these medical measures, educational measures must be brought into play as we shall discuss them below in reference to the generally retarded child. The same is true of children in whom general performance ability in no way corresponds to the good physical condition, as in the case of B 686, who showed good body control and good memory, in the face of generally poor performances (see Protocol, p. 260).

The most favorable prognosis is naturally to be made for those children who have both good physical development and good general performance ability, and the reliability of the prognosis depends upon the continuation of equally favorable or more favorable factors in their upbringing.

B. RETARDED AND WELL-DEVELOPED CHILDREN

Let us now consider individually the children designated as generally retarded or generally well-developed and in whose cases this judgment was not based solely upon good or poor physical conditions. We can distinguish among the retarded children two different kinds of cases—namely: *children in whom an actual retardation was found,* and children for whom the test results in no way agreed with the original judgment—that is, *children who had only the appearance but not the reality of retardation.* Under the actually retarded children there are those who show an *even retardation* along all separate lines. Their attainments in the handling of materials, for example, corresponds to their memory performance, to their ability in social contacts, to their imitativeness, to their body control. The test results have the appearance of that of a normal younger child. These cases seem to be the most hopeful. One might say that these were cases of delayed development, the cause of which was to be found in some inner or environmental hindrance. The following is an example:

G 666 C.A. 1 ; 1 D.A. 0 ; 11				
0 ; 8	0 ; 9	0 ; 10	0 ; 11	1 ; 0
+	+	+	+	—
+	+	+	—	—
+	+	+	—	—
+	+	+	+	—
+	+	+	—	—
+	+	+	—	—
+	+	+	—	—
+	+	+	—	—
+	+	+	—	—
+	+	—	—	—

In the majority of cases, however, the *retardation for the separate types of performance is very irregular.*

In some cases an *entire field of ability is missing,* a deficiency which rarely can be made up either with time or intensive educational measures. At all events, however, *the educator can turn to the test results for a statement of the talent-capital which he may count on in the child* and for a point of departure for his educational measures. The further advancement of a child will be difficult in cases such as that of B 686 where the *understanding for relationships* is in great part missing—in other words, where intellectual performance ability is very doubtful. Such cases can be recognized as early as the end of the first year in failure to fit hollow blocks into one another, to pull objects by their strings, to open the box, etc. B 841, C.A., 2 ; 3, a feeble-minded child with developmental age of 1 ; 5, who had the body control, social reaction, and memory ability of a child aged 1 ; 3 to 1 ; 9, was unable to understand the simplest connections which were required in the baby tests for the end of the first year. His inability to understand relationships of every kind showed itself in that he did not know any words to express his wishes, nor had he ever shown any decisive choice of a play-toy. In playing he occupied himself mostly with only one object because he was at a loss as to what to do with two things at the same time. This case also serves to show that the calculated developmental age alone tells very little, and that it is rather a more exact analysis of the passed and failed items which helps to give a clear picture of the child. In the case of children whose single performances deviate very greatly from one another we do not, as a general thing, take the calculated developmental age. This would be when the range of abilities of the child cannot be limited to the number of tests included in the normal child's span.[4] The case of B 841 is still more hopeful than that of B 692, C.A., 1;2, D.A., 1;0, whose physical development and imitative ability were good but, notwithstanding a minimal understanding for relationships, showed only very *weak memory* performances. He was unable to recall the contents of the box or the chicken even after the very shortest latent period. Also, the length of perseverance which was observed in his looking at a playtoy which had been taken from him consisted of only a very few seconds. Whereas B 841 must be termed capable of learning, there is little to be hoped for, even through practical habit-training in the case of B 692.

We attempted to accelerate the development of individually tested children by means of intensive educational measures. In those cases where the examination had shown complete absence of understanding of relations and very limited memory ability, our efforts were unsuccessful. However, *in the other cases in which we could count upon good memory performance, we were able to achieve good results* by making use of this ability. B 740 was a case of this sort. His developmental record as found in various tests follows:

Test 1	C.A. 2;2	D.A. 1;6
Test 2	C.A. 3;5	D.A. 1;11
Test 3	C.A. 3;9	D.A. 1;11
Test 4	C.A. 4;0	D.A. 2;4

We note here that between the second and third testings, without any discernible cause, a complete stand-

[4] *i.e.,* if he is unable to pass items in the lowest or can pass some beyond the highest of the team of five test series presented in the normal examination procedure.

still takes place in the development which, though slow, had been appreciable between the first and second testings. It was on this account that the child was given intensive care. The work of the psychologist, who spent several hours with the child three times a week, appears to have achieved results, for in the interval between the third and fourth testings the child made up markedly some of its deficiencies. The methods employed were drill and habit formation. These methods failed when applied to another case—namely that of B 745, who did not offer good memory, imitative ability, or the understanding of relationships as educational starting points. Unfavorable prospects for further development are also presented by *those children who, in addition to a lack in the understanding of relationships, are also unable to accomplish any imitation.* In our material we have cases of B 688 and B 819 of this sort. We are, at present, ready to state on the basis of measurement how significant it is for the child not to be able to understand relationships, to have a poor memory, and to be incapable of imitating, and also that it is not possible to develop such abilities where there is no tendency present. We also know how difficult any advancement of the child's development is when we are unable to count on these factors. We do not as yet understand the rôle which other less frequent deficiencies play. For example, we cannot say exactly what the following complete failure on the part of G 515, C.A., 1;0, means; she showed a marked retardation in the realm of body control and in all those items which tested affective development, such as the reaction to the withdrawal of a toy, to strange environment, to the sound of the bell, etc. (see Protocol, p. 261).

266

The Practical Reliability of the Tests

Many children who were proved by the tests to be retarded were observed to be *strikingly passive.* They were quite indifferent to the examiner and to the objects which they received for play. The examiner had to force the object upon them ten times or more before they would show any interest in it or grasp it. Their reaction times were very long. In many cases, to be sure, this passivity had already been observed by the doctor or the nurse, who had directed the child to be examined for this very reason. However, *passivity does not always mean retardation,* as is shown in those cases where children designated as retarded on account of their passivity show results in the tests quite in correspondence to their chronological age. An example of a case wrongly designated as retarded in this way is G 701, C.A., 1 ; 9, with a corresponding developmental age. The examiner, however, had to spend two hours on the test, whereas the average child takes only from a half hour to an hour.

G 701	1 ; 6	1 ; 9	2 ; 0
1	+	+	—
2	+	—	—
3	+	+	+
4	+	+	—
5	+	+	—
6	+	+	—
7	+	+	—
8	+	—	—
9	+	+	—
10	+	—	—

Although passivity is not necessarily the criterion of retardation and it is not true simply that all retarded children are passive, as we shall show, *passivity nevertheless constitutes a great danger for the child.* An active child seeks out the stimulation which he needs.

267

If he grows up in unfavorable conditions and does not receive the proper stimulation he will know how to obtain possibilities of action for himself; he will attract people's attention and therewith obtain opportunities for contact. The passive child, on the other hand, will remain idly seated if his toy has fallen, instead of grasping at the crib railing for want of another occupation and subjecting this to a thorough investigation, which is what his active comrade does. The passive child waits for stimulation and if this is not given him in representative measure, if people do not attend to him, direct him to activity with stimuli of various sorts, he is in danger of falling behind other children of his age.

Even as exaggerated passivity, *exaggerated activity can, on the other hand, become a disadvantage for the child.* In exact observation of children one will find that their activity can be directed to entirely different things. There are children who are very active in *social contact* and at the same time quite indifferent to *concrete material.* Others who show a great amount of activity in handling material are much more passive in social contacts. Finally, there is also a greater or lesser amount of *motor activity* observable in different children. Whether or not a child is active or passive in social contact, in handling of material, or whether he shows greater or lesser activity in general, and motor activity in particular, is a matter of great individual difference. Here, too, however, factors of development play an important rôle. A study of the activity of children reveals that this is at its strongest in social contact at the age of five and six months, but the nine months old child, in the grasping age, usually shows greater motor activity than activity directed toward people. The great motor activity which finds expression in the constant movement of the child is something very positive at eight months. If this activity, however, is predominant at a period in which the child should occupy himself receptively with material, in which he should look and listen, as in the case of the child of one year or older, this is to be regarded as a hindrance to his further development. The child in the second year of life who is constantly in movement becomes thereby incapable of receiving impressions. He will fail to look at the figure-card or his reflection in the mirror and will hardly notice the work of another. His constant movement will influence his performances in the field of imitation. He will not watch the examiner when she is showing him what to do. He will knock on the music-box with the sticks instead of beating the drum or turning the music-box. He will hardly be brought to building with blocks. However, this is not the place to discuss the single degrees of activity for each age-level. We have distinguished here *the different forms of material, social, and motor activity according to intensity,* and we can determine the degree of activity of the child in connection with the tests. A child very active socially, for example, is the one year old child who turns to the unfamiliar examiner as soon as she enters the room, tries to establish contact with her, "shows off" before her, puts away his playthings or leaves them unnoticed in order to devote himself to her, and constantly strives to get her to play with him. A less socially active child would quickly react to the stimulation of the examiner, immediately respond to organized play, follow commands, but would not of his own accord approach her and would overlook her were he engaged in some other activity. A child is socially inactive, finally, if he behaves quite indifferently to the examiner, who, by speaking with him and in other ways tries to engage him in social play, and who turns away from her and shows no interest for her at all.

Whether a child is active or passive is usually shown quite early. *The passivity of a child can be furthered by certain environmental influences*—for example, children who lack the necessary stimulation are often very passive. Passivity belongs in the picture of *institutional neglect* and *hospitalization,* which is lacking in the stimulation of the family life natural to this early age-level. This and other forms of *retardation depending upon environmental factors* can, in some cases, be recognized quite accurately in the testing. It is possible *to distinguish between naturally untalented children and those who have been influenced in this direction by the environment,* which fact is of great practical significance. The following are two examples in which harm is undoubtedly to be laid to the environment. In the case of G 855, C.A., o; 8, the physically weak child of a drunkard, who was taken away from the mother because her seven year old sister refused to care for her, the developmental age is o; 6; the test results showed performances in the field of bodily control to be good in so far as sitting, getting up, and locomotion were concerned; memory performance was likewise good. Poor results were found in performances calling for handling of playtoys and G 855 was unskilled at grasping. She failed consistently from the five months test on, in all items which tested ability at social contacts. The explanation is not hard to find as this was a neglected child who had no playtoys and no one to care for her. The older sister, as we later heard, was happy to go her own ways once she had dressed and fed the baby. In addition to the very limited opportunities for social contact the child had had unfavorable experiences with the mother who, in her drunken states, had screamed at her and frightened her.

G 855 C.A. 0;8 D.A. 0;6			
0;5	0;6	0;7	0;8
+	−	−	+
+	−	+	−
+	+	−	−
−	−	−	−
+	−	+	−
+	−	+	−
+	−	−	−
+	+	−	−
+	−	−	−
−	−	−	−

G 652 C.A. 1;11 D.A. 1;6			
1;0	1;3	1;6	1;9
+	+	−	−
+	+	+	−
+	+	−	+
+	+	+	+
+	−	−	−
+	−	−	−
−	−	−	−
+	+	−	+
+	+	−	−
+	−	−	−

Quite another picture is that of G 652, C.A., 1;11, who, on account of a rash, had been confined for months to a hospital bed and whose case was one of clear institutional neglect.

The case of G 652 can be summed up as follows: D.A., 1;6; good body control; great receptivity for social stimulation; the child only slightly active, and fearful (the test with the ball and the chicken, for example, could not be carried out because she was

271

frightened by the chicken) ; memory ability present, relations grasped. In spite of the great retardation we
were able to make a good prognosis for the child and
were not disappointed in this, as we shall show later.
The failure in many test items could be accounted for
by the lack of toys which the child had suffered during
the past months and by the limited possibilities for
contact. The memory ability and understanding of relations seemed to be valuable points of departure for
further development. In another case, that of B 686
and also that of B 841, we could not have made such
a favorable judgment. The results of a retesting of
G 652 at the age of 2 ; 4—that is, after five months—
showed that the child had made up almost the entire
retardation under the influence of good family care.
Her developmental age was practically the same as
her chronological age.

Similar to the cases where children designated as retarded are found in the tests sometimes to be actually
retarded and sometimes only apparently so, *there are
also among children termed accelerated those who are
actually so and those who only make this appearance.*
Examples for particularly well-developed children fol-

B 486 C.A. 0 ; 5 D.A. 0 ; 6				
0 ; 3	0 ; 4	0 ; 5	0 ; 6	0 ; 7
+	+	+	—	—
+	—	—	—	—
+	+	+	+	—
+	+	+	+	—
+	+	+	—	+
+	+	+	—	+
+	+	+	—	—
+	+	+	+	+
+	—	+	—	—
+	+	+	—	—

B 721	C.A. 1 ; 3	D.A. 1 ; 8		
	1 ; 0	1 ; 3	1 ; 6	1 ; 9
1	+	+	+	+
2	+	−	−	+
3	+	+	+	−
4	+	−	+	+
5	−	+	+	+
6	+	+	+	+
7	+	+	+	−
8	+	+	+	−
9	−	+	+	+
10	+	+	+	−

All cases in which the child was judged to be particularly well-developed without actually being so can be reduced to the one formula: It is always a case of children who are socially very active, who smile at the adult as soon as he comes near them and establish contact with him very easily. G 665 was termed very

G 665	C.A. 0 ; 11 + 6	D.A. 0 ; 11 + 0	
	0 ; 9	0 ; 10	0 ; 11
1	+	+	+
2	+	+	−
3	+	+	−
4	−	+	+
5	+	+	−
6	+	+	−
7	+	+	−
8	+	+	−
9	+	+	−
10	+	−	−

clever although her developmental age corresponded throughout to her chronological age. In as much as this is a special case, we have reckoned her age exactly to the number of days.

On the other hand, injustice is often done to those children whose social activity is weak and whose greatest activity and *highest achievements are in the field of manipulation of materials.* This type of activity is all too often overlooked. For example, G 856 C.A., 0; 8, was presented to us as a child not quite well-developed. The testing showed her to have a D.A., 0; 9, and an advance over her age was shown above all in her handling of materials. This child turned her attention intensively to material and to her playtoys, rather than to the observer.

Let us now ask ourselves whether *anything really new about the child can be stated on the basis of the tests,* or whether we can only corroborate the judgment of the practical observer. The practical value to be attached to tests will depend upon the answer to this question. *In twenty cases out of forty-five an examination was demanded because no clear judgment could be made of the child. In twenty-five cases the judgment had already been made on the child; the test results of seventeen of these cases agreed with this judgment, of eight cases disagreed.* We have already spoken of the errors of observation which can be made in the cases of passivity and of children who are socially particularly active. In the seventeen cases in which judgment of the parent or nurse agreed with the test results, we were able to state our judgment precisely, to measure the observed retardation or acceleration, and to determine in detail of what it consisted. We feel that this result speaks for the necessity of test examinations.

2. RESULTS OF RETESTING TWENTY-FIVE CHILDREN

As .has already been pointed out, the judgments which we make of children on the basis of test examinations often become decisive for their further life.

The Practical Reliability of the Tests

This is not only because the test results are made the point of departure for educational measures. Dependent also upon psychological judgment, along with the medical findings, are the answers to such questions as: Shall the child be left in his own family or given to foster parents? Shall he be placed in an institution for normal or for feeble-minded children? Shall he be adopted?—and many similar questions. The question now is: In how far does this judgment and prognosis of the further development of the child actually represent the facts? In order to determine this we began to subject children to a second examination after the lapse of a certain period of time, and we can now state some of these results.

In the case of twenty-five children, who were tested for a second time after a period of from four to twelve months (in the majority of cases after a period of six months), *the result of the first examination agreed with the result of the second* with the exception of two cases. The retarded child continued on a retarded level, the well-developed child again proved himself such, and the child who was representative of the average of his age again showed a D.A. corresponding to his C.A. The following table gives a few examples:

	First Testing			Second Testing		
	C.A.	D.A.	D.Q.	C.A.	D.A.	D.Q.
G 475	2 ; 0	0 ; 8	33+	3 ; 2	1 ; 1	34—
G 564	1 ; 11	1 ; 0	52+	2 ; 7	1 ; 7	61+
GA *	1 ; 2	1 ; 2	100	1 ; 11	1 ; 11	100
BC	1 ; 3	1 ; 6	120	1 ; 10	2 ; 7	114—
B 675	0 ; 9	0 ; 11	122	1 ; 0	1 ; 5	142—

* The children designated by capital letters were examined not with the general run of protocols but for particular scientific purposes.

As said before, only two children prove to be *exceptions*. B 646, the little boy with the curvature of the spine, who, when one discards the poor performances in the field of body control, first made a D.A. of 1;1 in the remaining fields, more nearly corresponding to his C.A. In the time intervening between the first and second testing he suffered from a serious case of intestinal trouble and was in a hospital under conditions which were injurious to his mental development, so that when he came up for retesting at the age of 1;5 a marked retardation was observed. The other case is that of G 652 whose first testing has already been discussed and whose retardation was found to be the result of environmental influences. The results of institutional neglect were completely made up for by helpful care within a family. At the time that she was given over to family care her C.A. was 1;11 and her D.A. 1;6; at the time of retesting her C.A. was 2;4 and her D.A. 2;4.

A boy, B 685, was found to have made no progress whatever during the four months intervening between the two examinations. During this time he was not ill, but lived in a condition of complete neglect on the part of his parents, who bothered very little about him. In as much as he is very passive and has a poor memory this developmental standstill is understandable.

There is no case in which the result of retesting directly contradicts our prognosis. The illness of B 446 could not have been foreseen, and in the case of G 652 we very decidedly assumed the harm to have been done by the environment and believed an improvement quite possible. In the case of B 685 we saw little possibility for development. Accordingly we found the accuracy of our prognoses to a great extent corroborated by the test results.

It is still to be noted that the absolute extent of retardation or acceleration in the case of one and the same child is by no means a constant quantity. In so far as the observations which we have permit us to judge, an acceleration of one month in the first year of life corresponds to one of three months in the second. In the case of retardations a comparison is not so easily seen. We cite the following examples of accelerated development:

	First Testing		Second Testing	
	C.A.	D.A.	C.A.	D.A.
G 548..	0;6 + 5	0;7 + 24	1;4 + 0	1;10 + 11
B 675..	0;9 + 12	0;11 + 3	1;0 + 18	1;5 + 12

With these figures we have proved that the test prognoses are reliable as concerns the near future of the child. How far this certainty will be determined with respect to longer periods of time will have to be proved by further retesting of these children and by a series of other investigations.

BIBLIOGRAPHY

ASCHAFFENBURG, G.—*Der Schalf im Kindesalter und seine Störungen.* Wiesbaden, 1909.

BECHTEREW, W.—*Allegemeine Grundlage de Reflexologie des Menschens.* Vienna. 1926.
Neues aus dem Gebiet der Reflexologie und Physiologie des Nervensystems. 1925.

BINET, ALFRED—*Le Developpement de l'Intelligence chez les Enfants.* 1908.

BÜHLER, CHARLOTTE—*Die Ersten Sozialen Verhaltungsweisen des Kindes. Quellen und Studien zur Jugenkunde. Heft 5.* Jena. 1927.
Kindheit und Jugend. Leipzig. 1928.

BÜHLER-HETZER-MABEL—*Affektwirksamkeit von Fremdheitseindrücken im Ersten Lebensjahr. Zeitschrift für Psychologie Band 107.* Leipzig. 1929.

BÜHLER and HETZER—*Über das Erste Verständnis für Ausdruck im Ersten Lebensjahr. Zeitschrift für Psychologie Band 107.*

BÜHLER and SPIELMANN—*Die Entwicklung der Körperbeherrschung bei Kind im Ersten Lebensjahr. Zeitschrift für Psychologie Band 107.* Leipzig. 1928.

BÜHLER, KARL—*Die Geistige Entwicklung des Kindes.*
Die Instinkte des Menschen. Bericht über den Neunten Kongress für Experimentelle Psychologie. Jena. 1925.
Krise der Psychologie.
Kritische Musterung der Neueren Theorie des Satzes. Indogermanic Jahrbuch VI. 1918.

CERNY—*Beobactungen über den Schlaf in Kindesalter Unter Physiologischen Verhaltnissen. Jahrbuch für Kinderheilbunde.*

DESCŒUDRES—*Le Developpement de l'Enfant de Deux à Sept Ans.* Paris, Neuchatel.

GESELL, A. L.—The Mental Growth of the Pre-school Child. Macmillan. 1925.

GOLDSTEIN—*Beobachtungen Über die Veränderungen des Gesamtverhalten bei Gehirnschaeigung Monoscraf. Pstrie und Neurol. 68.* 1928.

The First Year of Life

GUERNSEY, MARTHA—*Nachahmung in den Beiden Ersten Lebensjahren.* *Zeitschrift für Psychologie Band 107.* Leipzig. 1928.

HERZFELD and PRAGER—*Das Verständnis für Scherz und Komik in der Frühesten Kindheit. Zeitschrift für Angewandte Psychologie Band 32.* Leipzig. 1930.

HETZER—*Experimente über Konstruktive Betätigung.* In preparation. *Kindheit und Armut.*

HETZER-BEAUMONT-WIEHMEYER—*Das Schauen und Greifen des Kindes. Untersuchungen Über Spontanen Funktionswandel und Reizauslese in der Entwicklung. Zeitschrift für Psychologie Band 112.* Leipzig. 1930.

HETZER and KOLLER—*Eine Testreihe für das Zweite Lebensjahr.* In preparation.

HETZER and REINDORF—*Sprachentwicklung und Soziales Milieu. Zeitschrift für Angewandte Psychologie Band 29.* Leipzig. 1927.

HETZER and RIPIN—*Frühestes Lernen und Gegenstandserfassung bei Ernaehrungsvorgang. Zeitschrift für Psychologie Band 112.* Leipzig. In preparation.

HETZER and TUDOR-HART—*Die Frühesten Reaktionen auf die Menschliche Stimme. Quellen und Studien zur Jugenkunde Heft 5.* Jena. 1927.

JENNINGS, H. S.—The Behavior of the Lower Organisms. Columbia University Press. 1923.

JENSCHKE—*Nachprüfungen von Testprognosen.* In preparation.

KAUTSKY—*Kind und Spielzeug.* In preparation.

KLEIN—*Die Wirkung von Suggestion und Autorität bei Kleinkind.* In preparation.

KOFFKA—*Die Grundlagen der Psychischen Entwicklung.* 1925.

LAZARSFELD—*Über die Normierung entwicklungspsychologischer Daten. Zeitschrift für Psychologie Band 107.* Leipzig. 1928. *Statistisches Praktikum.* Jena. 1929.

LIPPMAN-BOGEN—*Naive Physik.* 1923.

LOWENFELD—*Systematisches Studium der Frühkindlichen Reaktionen auf Kläenge und Geräeusche. Zeitschrift für Psychologie Band 104.* Leipzig. 1927.

LUTTRINGHAUSEN—*Interesse und Neugier bei Kleinkind.* In preparation.

PARKER, G. H.—The Elementary Nervous System. Lippincott. 1919.

PINTNER, R. and PATERSON, D. G.—Scale of Performance Tests. Appleton. 1923.

PREYER, W.—Life of the Child. Appleton. Mental Development of the Child. Appleton.

Bibliography

STERN, W.—*Die Intelligenz der Kinder und Jugendlichen und die Methoden Ihrer Untersuchungen.* 3 Aufl. Leipzig. 1921.
Psychology of Early Childhood. Holt. 1924.

TERMAN, L. M.—Genetic Studies of Genius. I. 1924.
The Stanford Revision and Extension of the Binet-Simon Scale for Measuring Intelligence. 1927.

THORNDIKE, E. L.—Educational Psychology. Vol. II. Teachers College. 1913.

VOLKMANN—*Denkexperimente an Einjährigen.* In preparation.

WATSON, J. B.—Psychology from the Standpoint of a Behaviorist. Lippincott. 1924.

WISLITSKY—*Gedächtnis und Erwartung bei Kleinkind.* In preparation.

281

$\mathcal{C}$lassics $\mathcal{I}$n
$\mathcal{C}$hild $\mathcal{D}$evelopment

An Arno Press Collection

Baldwin, James Mark. **Thought and Things.** Four vols. in two. 1906-1915

Blatz, W[illiam] E[met], et al. **Collected Studies on the Dionne Quintuplets.** 1937

Bühler, Charlotte. **The First Year of Life.** 1930

Bühler, Karl. **The Mental Development of the Child.** 1930

Claparède, Ed[ouard]. **Experimental Pedagogy and the Psychology of the Child.** 1911

Factors Determining Intellectual Attainment. 1975

First Notes by Observant Parents. 1975

Freud, Anna. **Introduction to the Technic of Child Analysis.** 1928

Gesell, Arnold, et al. **Biographies of Child Development.** 1939

Goodenough, Florence L. **Measurement of Intelligence By Drawings.** 1926

Griffiths, Ruth. **A Study of Imagination in Early Childhood and Its Function in Mental Development.** 1918

Hall, G. Stanley and Some of His Pupils. **Aspects of Child Life and Education.** 1907

Hartshorne, Hugh and Mark May. **Studies in the Nature of Character. Vol. I: Studies in Deceit; Book One, General Methods and Results.** 1928

Hogan, Louise E. **A Study of a Child.** 1898

Hollingworth, Leta S. **Children Above 180 IQ, Stanford Binet:** Origins and Development. 1942

Kluver, Heinrich. **An Experimental Study of the Eidetic Type.** 1926

Lamson, Mary Swift. **Life and Education of Laura Dewey Bridgman, the Deaf, Dumb and Blind Girl.** 1881

Lewis, M[orris] M[ichael]. **Infant Speech:** A Study of the Beginnings of Language. 1936

McGraw, Myrtle B. **Growth: A Study of Johnny and Jimmy.** 1935

Monographs on Infancy. 1975

O'Shea, M. V., editor. **The Child: His Nature and His Needs.** 1925

Perez, Bernard. **The First Three Years of Childhood.** 1888

Romanes, George John. **Mental Evolution in Man:** Origin of Human Faculty. 1889

Shinn, Milicent Washburn. **The Biography of a Baby.** 1900

Stern, William. **Psychology of Early Childhood Up to the Sixth Year of Age.** 1924

Studies of Play. 1975

Terman, Lewis M. **Genius and Stupidity:** A Study of Some of the Intellectual Processes of Seven "Bright" and Seven "Stupid" Boys. 1906

Terman, Lewis M. **The Measurement of Intelligence.** 1916

Thorndike, Edward Lee. **Notes on Child Study.** 1901

Wilson, Louis N., compiler. **Bibliography of Child Study.** 1898-1912

[Witte, Karl Heinrich Gottfried]. **The Education of Karl Witte,** Or the Training of the Child. 1914